Walter Robson

The TWentieth-century WORLd

Oxford University Press   1995

Oxford University Press, Walton Street, Oxford OX2 6DP

Oxford New York
Athens Auckland Bangkok Bombay
Calcutta Cape Town Dar es Salaam Delhi
Florence Hong Kong Istanbul Karachi
Kuala Lumpur Madras Madrid Melbourne
Mexico City Nairobi Paris Singapore
Taipei Tokyo Toronto

and associated companies in

Berlin Ibadan

Oxford is a trade mark of Oxford University Press

© Oxford University Press 1995

First published 1995

ISBN 0 19 833563 6

Typeset by MS Filmsetting Limited, Frome, Somerset
Printed in Hong Kong

Acknowledgements

pp4, 5 (left & right) Hulton Picture Library; p5 Popperfoto (bottom left); p7 Imperial War Museum; p8 Popperfoto; pp11, 12, 13, 14, 15, 18 IWM; p19 Hulton Picture Library; pp20, 21, 22, 23, 24, 27 IWM; p28 IWM: C R W Nevison: The Harvest of Battle; p29 Hulton Picture Library; p30 IWM: Sir William Orpen: The Signing of Peace, Versailles, 1919; p31 IWM; p32 Peter Newark's Historical Pictures; p33 Hulton Picture Library; p34 Ullstein Bilderdienst ; p35 TASS (top left), Hulton Picture Library (bottom); p36 Igor Golomstock: Sergei Gerasimov: Festival in the Collective Farm; p37 IWM; p38 Hulton Picture Library; p40 IWM (top) copyright holder not known (bottom); p41 IWM; p42 Hulton Picture Library (top), IWM (bottom); p43 IWM (top left), Peter Newark's Military Pictures (top right); p44 Ullstein (top), IWM (bottom left); p44, 45 Hulton Picture Library (bottom & bottom right); p46-47 Peter Newark's Military Pictures; p47 IWM; p48 Ullstein (top left); p48-49 Popperfoto; p50 Daily Sketch (centre left), IWM (centre right), Ullstein (bottom right); p51 Ullstein (top), Hulton Picture Library (bottom); p53 & 54 Ullstein; p55 TASS (top), Ullstein (bottom); p56 Hulton Picture Library (centre right), IWM (bottom right); p57 IWM; p59 Hulton Picture Library; p60 Peter Newark's Military Pictures; p62 IWM (top), ET Archive/National Archive (bottom); p63 Ullstein; p64 ET/Signal; p65 IWM; p66 Camera Press; p67 Punch; p68 (bottom) Peter Newark's Military Pictures; pp68 (top), 69, 70, 71, 72 IWM; p73 Hulton Picture Library; pp74, 75 (bottom) IWM; p75 (top) & p76 Hulton Picture Library; p77 Popperfoto (top), Punch (bottom); pp78, 79, 80 (bottom) IWM ; p80 Hulton Picture Library (top); p81 Hulton Picture Library (top), IWM (bottom); p82 IWM, inset Camera Press; p83 Hulton Picture Library; p84 Ullstein; p85 Magnum; p86 Weiner Library (top), IWM (bottom); p87 Hulton Picture Library; p88 TASS, p89 IWM; p90 Hulton Picture Library; p91 IWM; p92 Rijksinstituut voor Oorlogsdocumentatie, Amsterdam; p93 IWM; p95, 97 (bottom left) Camera Press; p97 TASS (bottom right); p98 TASS; p99 Hulton Picture Library; p101 IWM; p102 Hulton Picture Library; p103 IWM; p104 Topham Picture Library; p105 IWM; p106 Hoover Institution Archives, Stanford University; p107 Camera Press; p108 The Source/Solo; p10 Stuart Heydinger/Observer/Camera Press; p110 Hulton Picture Library; p111 Ullstein; p112 Hulton Picture Library; p114 Ullstein; pp115, 116, 117, 118, 119 United Nations.

Cover picture *Troops in the Countryside* by Gilbert Spencer, by kind permission of Bradford Art Galleries & Museums/Bridgeman Art Library, London.

All illustrations are by Duncan Storr.

Contents

Preface

The title of this series is *Access to History*, and accessibility is its keynote – accessibility to National Curriculum History, in terms of both Programme of Study and Attainment Target.

The exercises, which refer to the text, sources, and illustrations, are intended to extend factual knowledge, promote comprehension, and develop a range of skills, all consistent with National Curriculum Key Elements. The 'criteria grid' (at the end of the book) shows how the individual exercises relate to the Key Elements.

It is not expected that pupils will work through the book unaided. Teachers will wish to omit some exercises and amend others. They will probably decide that some exercises which are set for individual work would be tackled more successfully by using a group or class approach, with the teacher him/herself as leader. The book's aim is to provide teachers with a useful set of resources, not to usurp their role.

The exercises with the fill-in blanks may be either photocopied to provide answer sheets and homework assignments, or copied out by the pupils and filled in as they go along.

From the Parade-ground to the Trenches

A They did not know the meaning of war

The two world wars of 1914–1918 and 1939–1945 caused 30 million deaths, and almost brought civilized life in Europe to an end. Men, women and children who lived through them found out how awful war had become. But *before* 1914 neither the rulers of the 'great powers' nor their subjects knew what modern warfare meant.

Source **1a**

Kaiser William II of Germany

Three of the six 'great powers' of Europe were ruled by **emperors**, who made all the big decisions themselves. In Germany and Austria–Hungary the emperor was called the **'Kaiser'**, and in Russia he was called the **'Tsar'**. Britain and Italy had kings, but they had to follow their ministers' advice. And France was a republic — it had no king at all.

The emperors often dressed in military uniforms, and spent a lot of time on parade-grounds, inspecting rigid lines of gleaming troops. But the soldiers were not just for show — they trained for war as well. And war was always present in the minds of the emperors and their ministers. As they argued over the map of Europe, and fell out about this or that province, threats of war were often in the air.

War was part of a great game to the rulers. And it was the same for men and women in the street. Wars made exciting news, and a victory was an excuse for a party. People did not realise that war meant dead soldiers, wrecked towns, and hungry children. But they soon learned. Before long, every family was mourning the loss of one or more of its young men.

Now try Exercise 1.1.

Source **1b**

Kaiser Franz Josef of
Austria–Hungary

Source **1d**

King George V of Britain knighting an admiral
aboard *HMS Princess Royal*

Source **1c**

Tsar Nicholas II of Russia with his son Alexis

Exercise 1.1

Read **Section A**, and look at **Sources 1a, 1b, 1c** and **1d**.
Then write notes on the great powers and their rulers,
answering these questions:

a Which were the great powers?
b Which three of them were ruled by emperors?
c What were the emperors' names?
d Which great power had neither an emperor nor a king?
e What do the sources tell us about how the emperors
dressed?
f Two of the rulers were first cousins. Who do you think
they were?
g What did the leaders of the great powers argue about?
h What threat did they often make when they fell out?

B The Alliances

In 1900, five of the six great powers belonged to **alliances**. Germany, Austria–Hungary and Italy were in one alliance, and France and Russia were in the other. Each alliance said that if one partner was attacked, the other(s) would come to its aid. This meant that a quarrel between two states could drag all five into war. And most of the great powers had large, and growing, armies.

Britain belonged to neither alliance. Her main concern was her **empire**, not Europe. But the empire led her into quarrels with the Russians and the French. For a time, it looked as though Britain would join the German side. But the British government was looking for peace. And in 1904 and 1907, it reached agreements with France and Russia on all the matters that could have led to war. And when France and Germany fell out over who should control Morocco in 1911, Britain took the French side.

Britain's main defence was her **navy**, which was the biggest in the world. So when the Kaiser started building German warships in 1897, it was seen as a challenge to Britain. Talks took place, but the Kaiser would not give up his plan, and the British would not let the Germans catch up. As Britain drifted away from Germany, she moved closer to France. After 1911, British and French navy chiefs made secret joint plans for war with Germany.

Now try Exercise 1.2.

Europe in 1914

M. Montenegro

Members of the Dual Alliance

Members of the Triple Alliance

Note: Italy was a member of the Triple Alliance, but it did not go to war on the side of Germany and Austria-Hungary in 1914. Instead, it joined the side of Britain, France, and Russia in 1915.

HMS *Dreadnought* in 1907. It was the first of a new class of British battleships which were bigger and more powerful than any other warships in the world. When Germany copied the *Dreadnought*, the pace of the 'naval race' quickened.

Source **1f**

It is not true that the German navy is a 'challenge to Britain's navy'. The German fleet has not been built against anyone. It is there to meet Germany's needs, above all to protect her growing trade. ... The British have a right to say that they need warships to defend their world-wide empire and trade. But it is not worthy of them to go on talking about the 'German danger'.

Adapted from a letter written by the German Kaiser in 1908.

Source 1e

The Germans are a great people, and they want to be strong on land and at sea. But to them, a navy is a luxury, while for us, the navy is essential. If we lost the command of the sea, our commerce would be destroyed and our industries would close down. But if German ships could not put to sea, they could still carry on their trade by land. So the stakes are not even. The Germans are playing for pride, and we are playing for our lives.

Adapted from an article in the *Daily Graphic*, 26 July 1909.

Exercise 1.2

Read **Section B** and **Sources 1e** and **1f**. Then write three paragraphs:

a According to **Source 1e**, **i** Why does Britain need to have the strongest navy in the world? **ii** Why do the Germans want a navy? **iii** Why do the Germans not need a large navy?

b According to **Source 1f**, **i** Why does Germany need a navy? **ii** What untrue charge has been made against the German navy?

c Why do you think the two sources disagree? What do they disagree about? Do they agree about anything?

People from ten different nations (Germans, Czechs, Poles, etc.) made up the empire of Austria—Hungary. So the Emperor was alarmed by the spread of **nationalism** in the Balkans (south-east Europe). Nationalism was the idea that each nation had the right to rule itself. If it took hold, multi-nation Austria—Hungary would fall apart.

The Austrians' chief worry was **Serbia**. (Look at the map on page 6.) The Serbs said that the people of **Bosnia** were Serbs, so Bosnia should belong to them. But in 1908 the Austrians made Bosnia part of their empire. The Russian Tsar objected — Russians looked on Serbs as their Balkan cousins. But when the German Kaiser backed the Austrians, the Tsar had to give way.

Then in 1912, Serbia and its allies in the Balkans fought and won a war with Turkey. Serbia got more land, and so became a bigger threat to Austria. So when in June 1914 the heir to the Austrian throne, **Franz Ferdinand**, was shot dead by a Serb in Sarajevo, the Austrians seized their chance. They sent a long list of demands to Serbia, hoping that the Serbs would refuse. Austria would then go to war, and crush Serbia for good.

As in 1908, the Tsar wanted to help the Serbs. He ordered his army to prepare for war with Austria. And when the German Kaiser tried to frighten him off, he stood firm. This was more than the Kaiser could take. He declared war on Russia on 1 August, and on France two days later. (The German generals *wanted* war before the French and Russian armies got any bigger.)

Archduke Franz Ferdinand and his wife setting out for their drive through Sarajevo on 28 June 1914

8

The quarrel grew into a world war because of the German plan for war with France and Russia. It said that the bulk of the army would be sent first to the west. It would march through **Belgium** into France, and win the war in the west in six weeks. Then it would turn east and deal with the Russians. But when the Germans invaded Belgium, **Britain** took the Belgian side. By midnight on 4 August 1914, Britain was at war with Germany.

Now try Exercises 1.3 and 1.4.

Exercise 1.3

Read **Section C**, then write out the events below in the correct order.

a Britain declared war on Germany.
b Archduke Franz Ferdinand was murdered in Sarajevo.
c Germany declared war on Russia.
d Bosnia became part of the Austrian Empire.
e The German army invaded Belgium.
f The Austrians sent a list of demands to Serbia.
g Germany declared war on France.
h The Russian Tsar ordered his army to prepare for war.

Source **1g**

In this most serious moment I appeal to you to help me. An unjust war has been declared against a weak country. The Russian people are angry, and I share their feeling. Soon I shall be forced to take measures which will lead to war. To try to avoid that calamity, I beg you in the name of our old friendship to do what you can to stop your allies from going too far.

Nicky.

Adapted from a telegram sent by Tsar Nicholas II of Russia to Kaiser William II of Germany at the end of July 1914.

Source **1h**

On account of our long and tender friendship, I am doing all that I can to reach a settlement with you. I am sure that you will help me to solve any problems that may still arise. Your very sincere and devoted friend,

Willy.

Adapted from Kaiser William II's reply to **Source 1g**.

Exercise 1.4

Read **Sources 1g** and **1h**, then answer the questions in sentences.

a Which words in the sources tell us that the Tsar and the Kaiser were on friendly terms with each other?
b Why were the Russian people (and the Tsar) angry?
c Which was the 'weak country' in **Source 1g**? Who had gone to war with it?
d Who were the Kaiser's 'allies' (**Source 1g**)?
e What did the Kaiser promise to do?
f Did the Kaiser agree that Austria was to blame for the crisis?
g What do you think the Kaiser wanted the Tsar to do?

2 The Western Front, 1914-1918

A The failure of the Schlieffen Plan

The German war-plan (the **Schlieffen Plan**) was nearly a success. In August 1914, five German armies marched through Belgium, wheeled to the left, and poured into northern France. The French and Belgian armies, and the 100,000 men the British sent to France, had to fall back before them.

Then, when some of their men were within sight of the Eiffel Tower, the Germans made a mistake — they let a gap open up between two of their armies. The French general seized his chance. He rushed men into the gap (some in Paris taxis), and beat the Germans in the **Battle of the Marne**. This battle saved the allies, and meant that the Schlieffen Plan had failed.

In the 'race to the sea' that followed, the Germans tried to capture the Channel ports (Calais and Boulogne). The allies held on to the ports, but by the end of 1914 most of Belgium and a large part of north-east France were in German hands. (Look at the Map.)

The Germans dug **trenches**, and set out to hold the land they had won. Opposite them, the allies also dug in, to stop any further German progress. Soon a complicated pattern of trenches — three or four lines on each side — stretched for 400 miles from the Belgian coast to the Swiss border.

Now try Exercise 2.1.

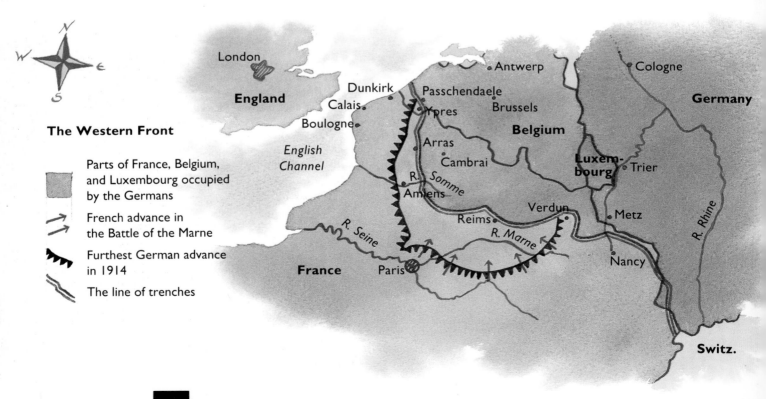

The Western Front

Parts of France, Belgium, and Luxembourg occupied by the Germans

French advance in the Battle of the Marne

Furthest German advance in 1914

The line of trenches

Exercise 2.1

Read **Section A** and look at the Map. Then copy out the sentences, filling in the blank spaces.

a Following the _____ Plan, the Germans invaded Belgium in August 1914.
b The Germans advanced into northern _____, and almost reached _____
c The Battle of the _____ in September 1914 was a great _____ victory.
d The allies stopped the Germans from taking the _____ ports.
e By the end of 1914, the Germans occupied almost all of _____
f Long lines of _____ soon stretched from the sea to the _____ border.

B Trench warfare

No words can properly describe the filth and horror of the trenches. Twisting earth-walled alleys, shored up with timber and sand-bags, and often partly filled with water, were where millions of young men lived and died. Dark, stinking dug-outs were where they took what little rest they got. A few hundred yards of 'no man's land', scarred with shell-holes and strewn with barbed wire, lay between them and the Germans.

Trench-life was a jumble of deafening noise, discomfort (from water, mud, rats, and lice), tiredness and fear. On quiet days, the men's time was split between duty on the fire-step, filling sand-bags and rest in the dug-out. When there was an 'offensive', everyone went 'over the top'. Going 'over the top' was dangerous at night, and close to suicide by day.

The allied generals hoped that the big guns would destroy the German trenches, and kill the men in them. When the guns stopped, the infantry would advance through no man's land and the German lines, and into the open country beyond. In fact, the German dug-outs were deep and strong. When the guns stopped, the Germans came out and manned their posts. And when the allied soldiers came in sight, the machine-guns mowed them down.

Trench warfare went on through 1915, 1916, and 1917. For five months in 1916, the Germans battered the French fortress of **Verdun**, at a cost of 600,000 killed and wounded. Sixty thousand British soldiers fell on the first day of the **Battle of the Somme** in 1916. And the British lost 320,000 men at **Passchendaele** in 1917. Was there no way out of the madness?

Now try Exercises 2.2 and 2.3.

Source **2a**

British soldiers filling sandbags with soil in a trench on the western front

Exercise 2.2

Read **Section B** and **Sources 2b** and **2c**, and look at **Sources 2a**, **2d** and **2e**. Write a short essay about trench warfare. Use the plan below:

a How long did the troops spend in the front line and in reserve? What were their duties? What did they do when they were off duty?
b What dangers and discomforts did the soldiers have to face?
c Do photographs tell us as much about the trenches as written sources?

Source 2b

The men of the working-party were building up the traverses with sandbags. [A traverse was a safety buttress in the trench.] ... The sentries stood on the fire-step, stamping their feet and blowing on their fingers. ... The German front line was about 300 yards away. From berths hollowed in the sides of the trench came the grunt of sleeping men.

Adapted from *Goodbye to All That* by Robert Graves, who was a junior infantry officer.

Source 2c

We stay in the front line eight days and nights, then have eight days' rest. At the front, the men are wet through much of the time. They are shelled and mortared, and even if they are not hit, they are always under a strain. They work all night, and a good part of each day, digging and filling sandbags – that is when they are not on sentry. The weather is icy, and the men can keep warm only when they are digging. When they sleep they freeze.

Adapted from a letter written by Lieut-Col Feilding in December 1916.

Source 2d

A British soldier standing on the fire-step, preparing to poke his head cautiously over the parapet

Source **2e**

British troops relaxing in the reserve trench, just behind the front line

Exercise 2.3

Read **Source 2f** and look at **Source 2g**, then answer the questions.

a Who first used poison gas?
b When and where was gas first used?
c What happened when the gas was released?
d Which sentence tells you that the gas was heavier than air?
e Why was the wind direction important in a gas attack?
f What were the effects of the gas?
g Why do you think that allied soldiers had no gas-masks at first?

Source 2f

Captain Bertram saw white smoke rising from the German trenches. Then in front of it appeared a green cloud, which drifted along the ground to our trenches. It rose only about seven feet from the ground. The men in our trenches were forced to leave, and a number of them were killed by the gas.

Adapted from a report in the *Daily Chronicle*, 29 April 1915.

Source 2g

British soldiers blinded by poison gas making their way to a dressing station. The Germans first used poison gas in the Battle of Loos in April 1915. It came as a complete surprise, and the allied troops had no gas masks. Later in the war the allies also used gas.

C Victory on the western front

Tanks were the British inventors' answer to the stalemate in the trenches. On the Somme, they had sunk into the soft earth and stuck. But when massed tanks were used on firm ground at **Cambrai** in 1917, they broke right through the German lines. The tanks' success surprised the generals, and they did not follow it up. So the Germans soon closed the gap again.

In 1917 there was good news and bad for the allies. The bad news was revolution in **Russia**. The Russians dropped out of the war, and the Germans were able to move men from the eastern front to the west. The good news was that the **U.S.A.** entered the war on the allied side. But the Americans took more than a year to enlist and train an army.

Ludendorff, the German commander, could see that Germany had to win the war in 1918 – before huge numbers of soldiers from the U.S.A. reached the western front. That is why he launched a massive offensive in March 1918. The allies were taken by surprise, and fell back again. Facing defeat, they agreed on a joint commander, the French general **Foch**.

In July the German advance came to a halt. The men were worn out, and there were no more reserves. The allies counter-attacked, and the Germans retreated. Ludendorff told the Kaiser that the war was lost, and that Germany must make peace. For the Germans, defeat was sudden and unexpected. The Kaiser fled to Holland, and Germany became a republic. The new rulers signed an **armistice**, or cease-fire, and the fighting stopped at 11 a.m. on 11 November 1918.

Now try Exercises 2.4 and 2.5.

British tanks fitted with 'cribs' for crossing German trenches – part of the allied advance in August–September 1918

> ### Exercise 2.4
>
> Read **Section C**, then write sentences to show that you know what these words mean:
>
> | | | |
> |---|---|---|
> | tanks | stalemate | revolution |
> | enlist | offensive | reserves |
> | counter-attack | armistice | |

14

Source **2i**

Canadian troops fixing bayonets before going 'over the top'

Exercise 2.5

Read **Source 2h**, and look at **Sources 2i** and **2j**. Discuss these questions in a group:

a In **Source 2h**, what are the facts? What has happened in the past week?
b What did Harry and Jack think of the general?
c What was the poet's opinion of the general and his staff?
d What facts about 'going over the top' can you learn from **Sources 2i** and **2j**?
e Did the artist who painted **Source 2j** have any opinions about the war?

Fact and Opinion

Facts are things that are true, or were true in the past. It is a fact that more than ten million men were killed in the First World War. An opinion is what someone thinks, believes or feels. In August 1914, it was many people's opinion that the war would be over by Christmas.

Source **2h**

*"Good morning; good-morning!" the General said
When we met him last week on the way to the line.
Now the soldiers he smiled at are most of 'em dead,
And we're cursing his staff for incompetent swine.
"He's a cheery old card," grunted Harry to Jack
As they slogged up to Arras with rifle and pack.
But he did for them both by his plan of attack.*

A poem by Siegfried Sassoon, who was a captain in the British army.

Source **2j**

'Over the top', a painting by John Nash

'Some corner of a foreign field . . .

3 The Eastern Fronts and the War at Sea, 1914–1918

Eastern and Central Europe, and the Near East

Norway
Sweden
St. Petersburg
Denmark
Baltic Sea
Latvia
East Prussia
Berlin
Russian Poland
Warsaw
Germany
Prague
Vienna
Budapest
Austria-Hungary
Italy
Romania
Serbia
M.
Bulgaria
Rome
Albania
Greece (G)
Moscow
Russia
Caspian Sea
Constantinople
Black Sea
'The Straits'
R. Tigris
Mesopotamia (Iraq)
Persia (Iran)
Baghdad
Syria
R. Euphrates
Cyprus
Palestine
Damascus
Persian Gulf
Mediterranean Sea
Suez Canal
Jerusalem
Arabia
Cairo
Egypt (British)
ARAB REVOLT
Red Sea
TURKISH EMPIRE

0   500 Km

Legend:

Neutral States

Germany, Austria-Hungary, and their allies

Allies of Britain and France

Other land conquered by the Germans and their allies

Parts of Russia occupied by the Germans and Austrians by the end of 1917

(G) ↗ Gallipoli landings, 1915

Furthest advance by Russian armies in 1914–1915

↗↗ British advances in Palestine and Mesopotamia (Iraq)

▲▲▲▲ Furthest advance by Germany and Austria-Hungary

M. Montenegro

Notes:
1 Bulgaria joined the German side in 1915, and helped to defeat Serbia.
2 Romania joined the Russians in 1916, but was soon defeated by the Germans and Austrians.

A The Russian front

To the Germans' surprise, two Russian armies marched into **East Prussia** in the first month of the war. In alarm, the Germans switched troops from their west front to the east. But before they arrived, the German armies in the east had beaten the Russians. The invasion threat was past.

Against the Austrians, the Russians had more success. Within a few months of the outbreak of war, much of the north-east part of the Austrian Empire was in Russian hands. But in 1915 the Germans, with Austrian help, drove the Russians back. By the end of that year the Germans were in control of all Russian Poland and Latvia. (Look at the Map.)

Russia suffered terrible losses in the first year of war. Four million men were killed, wounded or taken prisoner. But Russia was not short of men. What she lacked was arms — big guns, shells, rifles, and ammunition.

By 1916, the Russian factories were turning out more arms, and Britain and France were sending Russia all that they could spare. Boosted by these supplies, the Russians advanced into Austria. Again the Germans came to their allies' aid. When revolution broke out in Russia in March 1917, the armies were in retreat again.

Before the end of 1917, **Lenin** and the **Communists** were in power. And Lenin said that Russia must have peace, on any terms. The Germans took a huge slice of western Russia. Then, having won in the east, they turned to the job of finishing the war in the west. (See Chapter 2.)

Now try Exercises 3.1 and 3.2.

Exercise 3.1

Read **Section A**, then copy out the sentences and write TRUE or FALSE after each of them.

a It took the Russian army two months to get ready for war.
b The Russians invaded Austria–Hungary in the first months of the war.
c It was not until the end of 1916 that the Germans conquered Poland.
d By 1915 the Russian army was short of men.
e The British and French sent guns and ammunition to the Russians.
f Revolution broke out in Russia in 1917.
g Lenin was keen to continue fighting against the Germans.

Source   3a

As a rule, the army bakes its own bread — each corps has a bakery. In Poland in September 1914, though, the 9th Army bought bread from a civilian bakery. ... One unit, when it had no bread for five days in a row, gave each man 50 kopeks to buy bread — if he could!

Adapted from the diary of General Sir Alfred Knox, a British officer who was attached to the Russian army from 1914 to 1917.

Source   3b

May 1915 was the time when the shortage of arms was at its worst. In many units, soldiers were thrown into battle with no weapons. (They had to wait for comrades to be killed, then pick up their rifles.) The Russians were brave, but courage was not enough against the deadly German fire.

Adapted from a book written by Hugh Seton-Watson in 1967.

Source **3c**

Russian recruits marching to the front in 1916

Exercise 3.2

Read **Sources 3a** and **3b** and look at **Source 3c**. Then complete sentences **a** to **g** by choosing from the list on the right. Write out the complete sentences.

a General Knox spent three years ...

b There must have been times when ...

c Mr. Seton-Watson wrote his book ...

d The Russian shortages were ...

e Mr. Seton-Watson admired ...

f **Sources 3b** and **3c** both say that ...

g The Russian soldiers in **Source 3c** ...

- some Russian troops had no rifles.
- at their worst in 1915.
- on the Russian front.
- look quite happy to be going to war.
- the Russian troops got no food.
- 50 years after the Russian revolution.
- the bravery of the Russian soldiers.

B The Near East and the Mediterranean

Britain and France sent supplies of arms to Russia by sea. But the route through the Mediterranean and the Black Sea was closed when **Turkey** entered the war on the German side in October 1914. It was with the aim of knocking Turkey out of the war that the British decided to try to seize **'the Straits'**. (Look at the Map on page 16.)

But 'the Straits' were the hardest part of Turkey's empire to attack. When British, Australian and New Zealand troops landed near **Gallipoli** in April 1915, they did not get more than a short distance from the shore. They fought bravely, but the campaign was badly planned and badly led. It was a defeat for the allies, and a severe blow to Russia.

For three years, the British in **Egypt** were on the defensive against the Turks. It was only in 1917 that they advanced over the Suez Canal. Then in a few months they took all of **Palestine** and most of **Syria**. (They were helped by an Arab revolt against the Turks, led by 'Lawrence of Arabia'.) Further east, the British landed in the **Persian Gulf**, seized Baghdad, and gained control of the oil fields in what is now Iraq.

The British and French were pleased when **Italy** joined the allied side in 1915. They thought that the new front would keep an Austrian army busy. But the Italians suffered a massive defeat in 1917, and the allies had to send troops to help them and keep them in the war. A year later, though, an allied victory on the Italian front helped bring the war to an end and speed up the collapse of the Austro–Hungarian Empire.

Now try Exercise 3.3.

British gunners in Egypt defending the Suez Canal against the Turks

New Zealand troops landing at 'Anzac Cove'. Australian and New Zealand forces played a big part in the Gallipoli campaign and suffered heavy losses there.

Source 3d

On the cliff was a line of Turks shooting at us. The bullets came thick and fast, splashing up the water. As soon as I felt the boat touch, I jumped out into three feet of water, and rushed for the barbed wire on the beach. I got over it amidst a storm of lead and made for the cover of the sand dunes. I looked back. There was one soldier between me and the wire, and a whole line lying on the edge of the sands. The sea was crimson, and you could hear the groans through the sound of gunfire.

Adapted from a letter written by a Major Shaw in 1915.

Source 3e

The landing is almost over. All the troops and guns are on shore, and we have put them there without a hitch. ... I cannot help feeling proud at the manner in which the Navy have done their work. When I began the task I thought it was impossible. ... It was only when I realized that we had gained the cliffs and planted ourselves on the shore that I knew how much I had doubted our chance of success. How splendidly everyone worked!

Adapted from a letter written by Rear-Admiral Wemyss in May 1915.

Exercise 3.3

Read **Section B** and **Sources 3d** and **3e**. Then discuss these questions in a group. Record your group's answers on tape.

a The authors of **Sources 3d** and **3e** were describing the same campaign in the First World War — which campaign do you think it was? Which clues in the sources show that you are right?

b What differences **of fact** are there between the sources?

c Do both sources say what the authors' opinions were? How do you think the authors' opinions would differ?

d What **reasons** can you think of to explain the differences between the sources?

C The war at sea

When the war broke out in 1914, Britain imposed a **blockade** on Germany. This meant that the Royal Navy would stop or sink any ships that tried to enter or leave German ports. The results were shortages of food in German shops, and of raw materials (e.g. oil and rubber) in the factories.

For most of the war, the ships of the German High Seas Fleet stayed in port. The British Grand Fleet, at its base in the Orkneys, waited for them to come out. They did so only once, in May 1916. The outcome was the **Battle of Jutland** — a short fight which neither side won. After the battle, the Germans went back to port, and stayed there to the end of the war.

HMS *Invincible* sinking after the Battle of Jutland. The British lost more ships than the Germans in the battle, but the Germans did not risk another sea battle after Jutland. So both sides said they had won.

Exercise 3.4

Read **Section C** and the note on 'Causes', then answer the questions in sentences.

a What was the cause of the shortage of food and raw materials in Germany?
b Why did the German fleet remain in port for most of the war?
c Why did the Germans begin U-boat warfare in 1915?
d Why did the U.S.A. enter the war on the allied side?
e Why did the British start using the convoy system?
f Why did the allied navies win the war against the U-boats?

Causes

A **cause** is a **reason** for something. It is an answer to the question **Why?** – Why did it happen? Why were things like that?
For example: Why did the allies try to seize the Straits in 1915? Why were there such shortages of food and equipment on the Russian front?

In 1915, the Germans began their version of the British blockade. This was submarine, or **'U-boat'**, warfare. The German U-boats would surface close to allied merchant ships, sink them with torpedoes, and escape by diving under the waves. To win the war, though, the Germans needed to sink neutral as well as allied ships. And when their U-boats began sinking neutral ships in 1917, the **U.S.A.** joined in the war on the allied side.

In mid-1917, the U-boats were sinking so many ships that Britain was down to six weeks' supply of wheat. But when the merchant ships were ordered to sail in **convoys**, the number of sinkings fell. The convoys were protected by destroyers, which were equipped with hydrophones to detect U-boats, and depth charges to destroy them. If convoys had not been used, Britain might have had to drop out of the war.

Now try Exercise 3.4.

An allied merchant ship is hit by a torpedo. (This photograph was taken from the U-boat which fired the torpedo).

D The war in the air

The First World War broke out just eleven years after the first manned flight in a heavier-than-air machine. So it is hardly surprising that aircraft played just a small part in the war. What is important, though, is that this was the first war in which 'flying machines' played any part at all.

The planes of the **Royal Flying Corps** in 1914 were wood-and-canvas bi-planes. They carried one or two men at up to 70 m.p.h., and could go no higher than 10,000 feet. Their job was to fly over the German lines, spot gun positions, check movements of troops and supplies, and take photographs. They took off and landed just behind the allied lines, and were very much part of the army.

When rival airmen met, they tried to shoot each other down, at first with rifles and pistols. Out of these early duels grew the idea of the **fighter** plane, equipped with machine-guns. By 1918, both sides had fighters that could fly more than twice as fast and high as the planes of 1914. And scores of allied and German fighter pilots were fighting deadly 'dog-fights' high above the trenches every day. Very few of the pilots survived for more than a few weeks.

The aircraft of 1914 could carry one or two small bombs, which the crew would throw out when they were over the enemy lines. But as planes got bigger, they could carry more weight, so the **bomber** was born. As early as 1915, the allies were trying to bomb bridges, railways and arms dumps behind the German lines. And in 1917 and 1918, the Germans were making long-distance bombing raids on London, while the allies were bombing

'The Last Flight of Captain Ball', a painting by Norman Arnold

Cologne. Neither side did much damage, though, and bombers played no real part in winning the war.

The politicians in 1914 thought that flying was just a sport. But they changed their minds in the next four years. In 1918 the British government set up a brand new service, the **Royal Air Force**, to take over from the R.F.C. And by the end of the war, the R.A.F. had 22,000 aircraft (compared with the 64 that were sent to France with the British army in 1914). These were signs of things to come – some people could see that air-power would be vital in the future.

Now try Exercise 3.5.

Exercise 3.5

Read **Section D**, then make notes answering the questions.

a How was the First World War different from all previous wars, and why?
b How did the aircraft themselves change during the war?
c What was the task of aircraft at the beginning of the war?
d Two new kinds of aircraft were developed during the war – what were they?
e How did politicians' ideas about flying and air-power change?
Draw a picture of a First World War aeroplane.

4 The Home Front

Source **4a**

A nation at war

Cheerful, flag-waving crowds filled the streets of London in August 1914. By 1916 and 1917, though, the people were not so happy. They had learned that the whole nation was involved in modern war. And they found that the **government** controlled their lives much more than before.

For the first year of the war, Britain had a Liberal government, and **Herbert Asquith** was Prime Minister. But in 1915, Asquith asked Labour and the Conservatives to share the work of government, and join the Liberals in a **coalition**. Then in late 1916, when the war was going badly, a lot of M.P.s turned against Asquith. They forced him to resign, and got **David Lloyd George** to take over as head of the coalition government. And Lloyd George's energy and drive played a big part in winning the war.

As soon as the war began, the government called for **volunteers** for the army. (The peace-time army of 250,000 men was far too small.) So posters went up, urging men to enlist 'for King and Country'. Women were told to press their sons and husbands to join up (see **Source 4a**). Most of them did so, and some handed out white feathers to men who were not in uniform. The campaign was a great success — two million men volunteered by the end of 1914.

The flood of volunteers slowed down in 1915. And by 1916 the losses were so heavy that the army was short of men. So the government started **conscription** — men between 18 and 41 were compelled to enlist. Only workers in vital industries (e.g. arms-making and coal-mining) were exempt.

Women took over a lot of jobs when the men went to war. They worked on farms, drove buses and trams, cleaned windows, and 'manned' the fire brigade. Others made guns, shells and tanks in the factories, worked as clerks in government offices, or joined the new women's services. Hundreds of thousands of women served as nurses, some on the front line in France.

Now try Exercises 4.1 and 4.2.

Exercise 4.1

Read **Section A**, then write three paragraphs about **Changes during the War**. Use the headings and questions below as a guide:

a The people: What did they learn? Was there a change in what they thought about war?

b The government: Was there a change in its powers? Was there a change of Prime Minister? Was there a change of party in power?

c The army: What change took place in the size of the army? Were there always plenty of volunteers? When and why did conscription begin?

Exercise 4.2

The text of **Section A**, plus **Sources 4a**, **4b**, **4c** and **4d**, will help you to answer the questions below. Write your answers in sentences.

a **Source 4a** asks women to do what to help recruiting?

b How did some women try to shame men into joining the army?

c **Sources 4b**, **4c** and **4d** show women doing which jobs?

d Which other jobs, not shown in the sources, did women do during the war?

e Why do you think there was a fall in the number of women who had paid jobs when the war ended?

f What do you think men said about women and the work they did in the war?

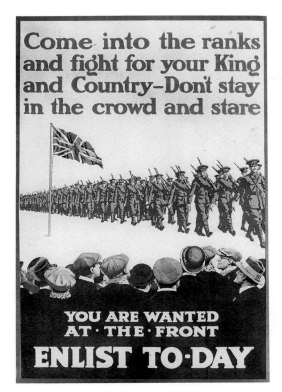

Come into the ranks and fight for your King and Country—Don't stay in the crowd and stare

YOU ARE WANTED AT·THE·FRONT

ENLIST TO·DAY

A recruitment poster appealing to men's patriotism

Source 4b

Female workers in an arms factory

B Ration-books and Zeppelins

The war was a monster which consumed men. It took women's husbands and children's fathers, often for good. It made country children into wage-earners — they left school at eleven or twelve to work on the land. In town schools, boys' classes were taken by women. Some boys and girls had part-time schooling, sharing their schools and teachers with other children.

The German U-boats (see Chapter 3) caused a food shortage in Britain, but not a famine. The bread turned a strange colour, because it was made from a mixture of wheat and potatoes, and butter vanished from sight. But **rationing** did not begin until 1918. Helpful experts advised people to chew their food slowly to make it last longer!

A Zeppelin

For the first time in history, Britain itself was bombed and shelled. The first taste came in late 1914, when three towns in the north-east were shelled from the sea. Then came raids by **Zeppelins** (gas-filled airships) and, in 1917 and 1918, bombing raids by German aeroplanes. A total of 1,400 civilians were killed.

In the days before radio, the news came from newspapers, and **rumours**. The government could control the press, but not the rumours. So stories went round about the thousands killed in Zeppelin raids, and the awful deeds of the German army in Belgium. But there was also good news, such as that Russian troops had landed in Scotland, on their way to the western front. (You could tell they were Russians by the snow on their boots!)

Now try Exercise 4.3.

Source **4e**

The cotton mills had always employed far more women than men. So the loss of men to the army affected the cotton industry less than others. But to get more cheap labour, the mill-owners wanted children to start work as part-timers at eleven years old, instead of twelve. And they wanted them to start full-time work at twelve, instead of thirteen.

Adapted from *The Home Front*, by Sylvia Pankhurst.

Source **4f**

*London's anger at the sinking of the **Lusitania** burst in a storm yesterday. Shops owned by Germans were pillaged by huge crowds which the police were not able to control. ... Some German butchers who turned up at Smithfield were mobbed and thrown out of the market by the meat porters. Another German was chased all the way to Holborn by a crowd of 300 — every office-boy in the district joined in.*

Adapted from a report in the *Daily Mirror*, 13 May 1915.

Source **4g**

One morning in the early summer of 1916, ten or twenty German bombers appeared over London. They looked like gnats. We rushed to the roof of the warehouse where I worked to watch. They dropped a few bombs, killed some horses in Billingsgate, and turned Cheapside into a river of broken glass. ... On this morning, Great Britain ceased to be an island.

Adapted from a book written by V. S. Pritchett in 1962.

Exercise 4.3

Read **Section B** and **Sources 4e**, **4f** and **4g**. Then discuss the questions below in a group. Make a tape recording of your group's answers.

a When had children started work in the cotton mills before the war?

b When did the mill-owners want the children to start work?

c What did the author of **Source 4e** think of the mill-owners?

d Who do you think the Germans mentioned in **Source 4f** were?

e Which **facts** in **Source 4f** show that Germans were badly treated?

f Which event had made the Londoners so anti-German?

g Can you tell anything about the reporter's opinions in **Source 4f**?

h Facts from **Source 4g**: When did the raid occur? How many bombers were there? How many bombs did they drop? How much damage did they do?

i What does 'a river of glass' mean? Where had the glass come from?

j What was the opinion of the author of **Source 4g**?

C 'A land fit for heroes'?

If it was a people's war, what did the people get out of it? Lloyd George said that his government's aim was to make Britain 'a land fit for heroes'. And the first thing that the 'heroes' got was the right to vote for their leaders. In 1918, Parliament passed an act which gave the vote to **all** men over 21, and to men **under** 21 who had fought in the war.

But women had also played a big part in the war. And Parliament recognized that fact when it gave some women (those over 30) the vote as well. So while the campaign for 'Votes for Women' before the war had failed, women's war work had won the M.P.s (who were all men) over to the women's cause.

Germany and the U.S.A. also gave women the vote at the end of the First World War. But women in France had to wait until 1945.

What about the children of the 'heroes' and 'heroines'? Before the war, some boys and girls left school at twelve or thirteen. And during the war, many children got even less schooling (see Section B). But an act passed in 1918 paved the way to a better system of education. It said that all children would stay at school at least to the age of fourteen. It also promised part-time education after fourteen, but that was one of the promises that were not kept.

The 'heroes' needed homes and work. It was soon clear that there were not enough jobs, and that the government could not find work for everyone.

It did try, though, to help the unemployed, when it said that all workers without jobs were entitled to 'the dole'. It also tried to deal with the shortage of houses. It helped local councils to get rid of slums and build new, solid homes – the first 'council houses'. But money was short, so not enough houses were built, and the 'dole' was always a very small amount.

And were the people grateful? At first they were – the leaders got the credit for winning the war. Then unemployment and poverty changed the people's mood. More working men joined trade unions than ever before, and more working days were lost in strikes. And in 1924, for a few months, the **Labour Party** for the first time formed the government of Britain.

Now try Exercise 4.4.

Exercise 4.4

Read **Section C**, and find facts which answer the questions. Write your answers as a set of notes.

a What did the government promise?
b What did it do about voting rights, education, housing and the unemployed?
c What more could the government have done? Why did it not do more?
d What did the people think?

D Germany in war-time

Before the war, the **Kaiser**, not the people, chose the government in Germany. But as soon as the war began, the army took command. For the last two years of the war, General **Ludendorff** was almost a dictator.

Germany had conscription even in peace-time. All young men had to do a period of service in the army, followed by a spell in the army reserve. When war broke out, those under 40 had to report for duty. And a law passed in 1916 said that men up to 60 could be called on to serve, either in the army or in the arms factories. The law applied just to men, but women and children were urged to take jobs to help the war effort.

Because of the British blockade, German factories were short of raw materials. But the army's conquests put the coal and iron of Belgium and north-east France into German hands. And German inventors found ways of making cloth from wood-pulp and aluminium from clay. They even discovered how to make nitrates (for fertilizers and explosives) from the air.

What inventors could not overcome was the shortage of food. Bread was rationed from 1915, and most other foods soon followed. There was no real hardship, though, until the winter of 1916–1917. Then an early frost killed the potatoes, and the people had to live on turnips. By 1918, food supplies for the poor were really short. (The rich could buy meat, coffee and sugar at three times the normal price on the **'black market'**.)

Now try Exercise 4.5.

German soldiers leaving home at the beginning of the war

Exercise 4.5

Read **Section D**, and try to find in it words or phrases which mean the same as the phrases below:

a A ruler who can do exactly as he likes.
b Compulsory army service.
c Ex-soldiers who can be called up again in time of need.
d Using warships to stop merchant ships going into or out of ports.
e Goods such as coal, iron ore, rubber, and oil.
f Scientists who were trying to solve the war-time problems.
g Chemicals that are put on the land to make it more fertile.
h Illegal trade in scarce goods.

The people of Germany were so hungry in 1918 that they rioted and looted the food shops. Here you can see soldiers on guard outside the shops to prevent further looting.

5 The War to End Wars

A Winners and losers

C.R.W. Nevinson's painting shows soldiers of both sides making their way home across the battlefields of the First World War

At eleven in the morning of 11 November 1918 the killing stopped. The war was over. (We call it the **'First World War'**, but at the time it was just the **'Great War'**.) Britain and France, helped by Italy and the U.S.A., had 'won'. Germany and her allies, Austria and Turkey, had 'lost'.

In fact, there were far more losers than winners. The thousands who lost arms or legs were losers. So were the victims of poison-gas, and the young men whose nerves were shattered by exploding shells. The mothers who gave their sons were losers. So were the wives whose husbands did not come home, and the children left with no fathers. And there were as many losers in France and Britain as in Germany.

More than ten million men died in the four years of war. The soldiers who survived could hardly believe their good luck. Many of them even felt uneasy when the guns fell silent — their bodies and minds had got used to the constant din and the knowledge that the next minute might be their last.

When the truth sank in, they wanted to go home. Their deepest hope was that no-one would be called on to go through the same again.

Politicians called it 'the war to end wars' — it was so awful that there must never be another war. Most of them meant what they said. Some of them could even see that it was the pride, ambition and folly of the rulers and politicians that had caused the war. What they could not do was agree on a way to keep the peace.

Now try Exercise 5.1.

Exercise 5.1

Read **Section A**, then copy out the following sentences and write TRUE or FALSE after each one.

a The First World War ended on 11 November 1918.
b The U.S.A. was on the side of Britain and France in the First World War.
c Italy was on Germany's side in the First World War.
d Poison-gas was not used in the First World War.
e Over ten million men were killed in the First World War.
f It took some time for the soldiers to realise that the war was over.
g The politicians learned nothing from the war.

B Peace

In 1914, when the war began, Europe had three emperors. By the end of the war they were all gone. The Tsar gave up his throne in the Revolution in 1917. The Austrian Empire fell apart and Germany became a republic just before the fighting ended.

The world's leading statesmen met in Paris in 1919 to make and sign peace treaties. **David Lloyd George** for Britain, **Georges Clemenceau** for France, and **Woodrow Wilson** for the U.S.A. took all the big decisions. No Germans, Austrians, or Russians took part.

Clemenceau said that Germany had started the war when it invaded Belgium in 1914. So he thought that Germany should be punished, and made so weak that she could never go to war again. Wilson wanted to prevent future wars by setting up a **League of Nations**, which would settle quarrels between states. And he thought that all peoples should have their own states — Poland for the Poles, Denmark for the Danes, etc.

In the **Treaty of Versailles**, the statesmen made new states for the Poles, the Czechs and Slovaks, the Yugoslavs, etc. They also decided that Germany must be punished. They took land from her, and said that she had to pay for the damage her armies had caused. They cut down her forces, and banned her from keeping troops in the Rhineland (on her western borders).

And they set up a League of Nations to keep the peace. The idea was that if one state attacked another, all the other members would force it to stop. If the League was to work, though, all the leading nations had to back it. But the U.S.A., the world's strongest nation, refused to join the League.

Source 5a

The world's leading statesmen at the peace conference: Georges Clemenceau (left), Woodrow Wilson (centre), and David Lloyd George (right)

The first meeting of the League of Nations in November 1920

Now try Exercises 5.2 and 5.3.

Source **5b**

'Bring in the Germans', said Clemenceau, in a harsh, loud voice. Two ushers appeared through the door at the end of the Hall of Mirrors. After them came four officers. Then came the Germans, Dr. Müller and Dr. Bell. The silence was terrifying. Their feet echoed on the wooden floor. ...Two thousand staring eyes were on them. They were deathly pale — one of them thin, and the other moon-faced. We all found it very painful.

Adapted from a book written by Harold Nicolson in 1933.

Exercise 5.2

Read **Section B** and **Sources 5b** and **5c**, and look at **Source 5d**. Read the note on 'Primary and secondary sources'. Answer the questions in sentences.

a Who wrote **Source 5b**, and when?
b Which sentence in **Source 5b** proves that it is a primary source?
c Who wrote **Source 5c**, and when?
d Is **Source 5c** a primary source or a secondary source?
e Who painted **Source 5d**?
f Is **Source 5d** a primary source or a secondary source?

Primary and secondary sources

Books written by people who were present when events happened are primary sources. Records of speeches, photographs, and paintings by artists who were there are also primary sources.
Books written by people who were not present are called **secondary sources.**

Source **5c**

The Foreign Minister, Hermann Müller, and the Minister of Justice, Johann Bell, travelled to Versailles. On 28 June (1919), they signed the treaty in the Hall of Mirrors.

Adapted from a book written by Dr. William Carr in 1969. Dr. Carr was not present when the treaty was signed.

Source **5d**   Sir William Orpen's painting of the signing of the Treaty of Versailles. The artist was present when the Treaty was signed.

Exercise 5.3

What can we learn from **Sources 5b**, **5c**, and **5d** about the signing of the Treaty of Versailles? Note down facts about

a the room where the Treaty was signed.
b the people present when the Treaty was signed. (If you look at **Source 5a**, you will be able to name some of them.)
c the Germans who signed the Treaty.
Say which source each of your facts comes from.

The peace treaty said that most of the German navy had to be handed over to Britain. The ships sailed to Scapa Flow in the Orkneys, where their crews scuttled them. This is the Battle Cruiser Hindenburg after being sunk.

C Germany's complaints

The Treaty of Versailles, which ended the war with Germany, was supposed to be fair and just. It did not seem fair and just to the Germans, though. And German complaints about the unfair Treaty helped to cause the next war, twenty years later.

Firstly, they complained that no Germans took part in the discussions. The winners drew up the Treaty, and forced the Germans to sign. Secondly, if each nation was to have its own state, why could the Germans not have theirs? Why were the Germans of Austria not allowed to join Germany? And what about the Germans who lived in Czechoslovakia and Poland?

Europe after the Treaty of Versailles (1919)

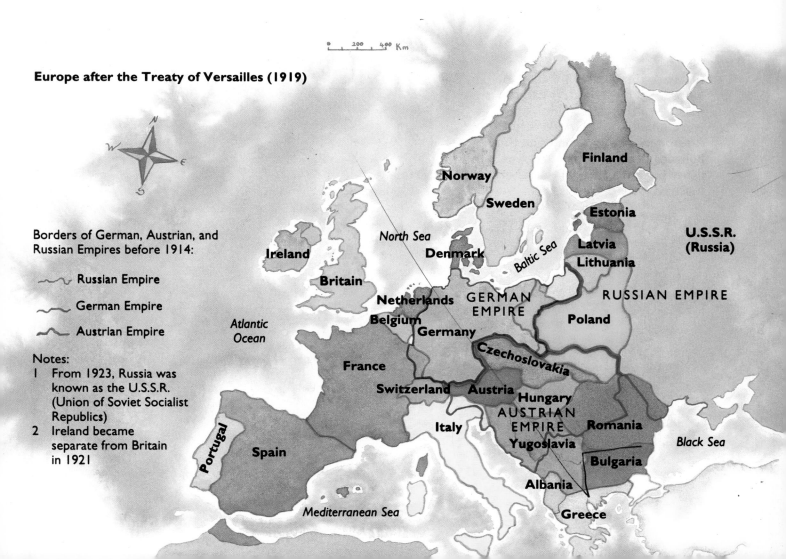

Borders of German, Austrian, and Russian Empires before 1914:

~~~ Russian Empire

~~~ German Empire

~~~ Austrian Empire

Notes:
1 From 1923, Russia was known as the U.S.S.R. (Union of Soviet Socialist Republics)
2 Ireland became separate from Britain in 1921

Thirdly, the great statesmen talked about 'disarmament' as a way to keep the peace. But the only state that was disarmed in 1919 was Germany. (Her army was cut down to 100,000 men, and she was allowed no tanks or submarines, and no air force.) The Germans asked why the French army and the British navy were not cut down as well.

Worst of all for the Germans was the fact that they were blamed for causing the war. They had to pay the allies for all the damage done by their armies. The Germans said that they were not the only ones to blame. They said that the statesmen of all the nations caused the war. And they said that they could not afford to pay the huge amounts that the allies wanted.

Now try Exercises 5.4 and 5.5.

Fact and opinion

Facts are things that are true, or were true in the past. It is a fact that more than ten million men were killed in the First World War. An opinion is what someone thinks, believes or feels. In 1919, it was many people's opinion that there must be no more wars.

Source 5e

I knew then that all was lost. Only fools, liars and criminals could hope for mercy from the enemy. Hatred grew in me for the politicians who signed the surrender. The more I thought about it, the more the shame and disgrace burned me. What was all the pain in my eyes compared to this misery? At once, I knew my fate – I must go into politics.

Adapted from Adolf Hitler's book, *Mein Kampf*. Hitler was in hospital in November 1918 – he had been gassed in the trenches.

Source 5f

An English general said that the German army was stabbed in the back. He was right. You can not blame the army. The officers and men fought well. It is clear that the politicians who made the peace are to blame for this disgrace.

Adapted from the words of Field Marshal Hindenburg, who was head of the German army in 1918–1919. Later he was President of Germany.

Exercise 5.4

Read **Section C** and **Sources 5e** and **5f**. Read again the note on 'Fact and opinion' on page 15. Write a paragraph about each of the sources, answering these questions:

a Which facts can you find in **Source 5e**? What were Hitler's opinions?
b What is the only fact in **Source 5f**? What were Hindenburg's opinions? What facts do you know about Hindenburg?

Exercise 5.5

Write sentences to show that you know what these words mean:

ally   emperor   republic   statesmen   treaty
disarmament   submarine

An election poster from the 1930s featuring Hitler and Hindenburg

6 Democracy and Dictatorship

A The democracies

In 1918, Britain, the U.S.A., and most countries in Europe were **democracies**. This means that their governments were chosen by the people, in elections held every few years. All men (and in some cases women too) had the right to vote. Free speech, and a free press, meant that men and women were not locked up for speaking their minds.

The problems these governments had to face were huge. The north-east of France had been laid waste by war, and the French expected the Germans to pay to put things right. The German government had borrowed from its own people to pay for the war, and now was deeply in debt. Its money problems grew so bad that in 1923 the German **mark** became worthless. (At one time in 1923, there were 16,000 million marks to the pound.)

But the countries of Europe and the U.S.A. helped each other, and began to solve their problems. The Germans borrowed money from America. The French agreed to ask for no more than the Germans could afford. All the states of western Europe promised not to go to war with each other again.

Then in 1929 came the **Wall Street Crash**. The value of stocks and shares in the U.S.A. took a sudden fall. Americans who had lent money to Germany wanted it all back. Trade took a nose-dive, and by 1932 there were three

million unemployed in Britain, six million in Germany, and thirteen million in the U.S.A. The governments of Britain, France, and the U.S.A. just managed to cope. But by 1933, democracy in Germany was dead.

Now try Exercises 6.1 and 6.2.

In 1923 German money became almost worthless. Above is a single banknote for two million marks. By the end, children were using piles of banknotes as toys!

Exercise 6.1

Find words and phrases in **Section A** which mean the same as the groups of words below:

a Government chosen by the people in free elections.
b Newspapers free to print the news as they wish.
c Owed very large sums of money.
d German money.
e A sudden fall in the prices of stocks and shares in New York.
f People who have no jobs.

Source 6a

When the Germans stopped making payments to the French in 1923, the French army moved into the Ruhr (Germany's main industrial area). Here you can see a French armoured car in the street of a Ruhr town.

Source 6b

There are some who mock the League of Nations and say that it is bound to fail. What will they think now? From now on, there will be peace for France and Germany. That means that we have done with the long series of bloody wars that have stained the pages of history. All countries must learn that if they give up a little of what they want, they win the greater prize of world peace.

Adapted from a speech made by Aristide Briand, the French Foreign Minister, in 1926. He made the speech soon after ministers from Britain, France, Germany and Italy had signed a treaty at Locarno in Switzerland. In the treaty, they promised never to go to war again.

Deductions from the sources

The sources do not always tell us everything we would like to know. But we can often make **deductions** from the sources (work out things from the clues we have). For example, the photograph on page 33 shows German children playing with bundles of banknotes. We can make the deduction that the notes were of little or no value.

Exercise 6.2

Read **Source 6b**, and look at **Source 6a**. Read the note on 'Deductions from the sources'. Then copy out the sentences and write TRUE or FALSE after each of them.

a **Source 6b** tells us that some people were against the League of Nations.
b Aristide Briand was against the League of Nations.
c Briand thought that, after the Locarno Treaty, there would be peace between France and Germany.
d Briand hated war.
e French troops patrolled the streets of some German towns in 1923.
f The Germans were pleased to see the French soldiers.
g German railway workers went on strike and no trains were running.
h The French army expected trouble from the Germans.

Some of the statesmen who met at Locarno in Switzerland in 1925, including: Stanley Baldwin, Winston Churchill, and Austen Chamberlain of Britain; Aristide Briand of France; Edward Benes of Czechoslovakia and Gustav Stresemann of Germany

B Communist Russia

The Tsar of Russia could not deal with the demands of the First World War. Famine in the towns led to strikes and riots. The soldiers were short of boots, clothes, and weapons, and they began to desert. The Tsar fell from power in March 1917. By the end of the year, **Lenin** and the **Communists** were in charge.

Lenin made peace with the Germans. He fought and won a civil war against the supporters of the Tsar. And he began to bring in Communism — some factories and shops were taken over by the state. **Stalin**, who became the leader when Lenin died in 1924, went much further. He made the peasants give up their land and join huge '**collective farms**'. And with his '**five year plans**', he turned Russia into a modern industrial state.

Russia became a **one-party state** — only one party was allowed, in this case the Communists. Lenin and Stalin were **dictators**, or rulers with complete power. Those who tried to resist them were sent to prison or labour camps. Peasants who opposed Stalin's plan to take away their land were starved into giving way. (More than three million peasants died.)

Stalin's secret police had spies everywhere. People did not trust their neighbours. Everyone waited in dread for a knock on the door in the middle of the night. In the 1930s, even the top Communists were put on trial. They 'confessed' to amazing crimes, such as plotting to murder Stalin and to commit treason. All were sentenced to death — Stalin was getting rid of his rivals.

Now try Exercise 6.3.

A Communist parade in Red Square, Moscow in 1937. The banner reads 'We love Comrade Stalin, the leader of the peoples of the U.S.S.R.'.

Source **6c** Russian peasants waiting for bread during the famine of 1921

Exercise 6.3

Read **Section B**, and study **Sources 6c** and **6d**.

a What differences can you see between the two pictures? Write a paragraph comparing them. Do the peasants look hungry or well-fed? Are they clean or dirty? Do they seem miserable or happy? Is there any food and drink to be seen? What are the peasants doing?

b Here are some possible reasons why there are differences between the sources. Copy them out and fill in the blank spaces.

   i Source _____ is a photograph, so what it says must be _____

   ii Source _____ is a painting. The artist was possibly told by the _____ to make the peasants look _____

   iii The photograph was taken in _____, and the picture was painted in _____

   iv There was a _____ in 1921, but not in 1937.

C Dictatorship in Italy and Japan

In 1922, a dictator came to power in **Italy**. This was **Benito Mussolini**, who called himself a **Fascist**. Like Stalin, he wanted a one-party state, but in his case the Fascists were the only party allowed. Like Stalin, he was fond of parades and rallies, with flags and speeches. And he too had his enemies beaten up, jailed, or killed.

On the other side of the world, **Japan** claimed to be a democracy in the 1920s. Men, but not women, had the right to vote there. And more than one party was allowed. But the leaders of the parties were not honest, and did not win the people's respect. And after the Wall Street Crash in 1929, Japan was hit by the fall in world trade.

Democracy got the blame for the slump in Japan — the man in the street wanted a job and a wage, and did not care much for votes and parties. In Japan, though, it was not one man or party that came to power, but the **army**. The officers said that they alone were loyal to the emperor and stood for the honour of Japan. And when they took control, the people were on their side.

Mussolini and the Japanese saw themselves as warriors. The Japanese wanted to take over parts of **China**. Mussolini pictured himself as the man who would rule the **Mediterranean**. And he longed to conquer an empire in **Africa** as well. These two states were prepared to fight for what they wanted. Already they had forgotten the lessons of the First World War.

Now try Exercise 6.4.

Source **6d**

A Russian picture painted in 1937. It shows the workers on a collective farm. They are listening to a speech telling of all the good things the Communists have done.

Benito Mussolini making a speech

Source 6e

For the first ten years of his rule, it seemed that he had no ambitions in Europe or in Africa. When he went abroad, he dressed in a butterfly collar and spats, top hat, white gloves, and badly pressed trousers. He did not look like the fierce dictator that people expected. They were surprised by his smallness, too, and by the warmth of his smile. Lord Curzon said, 'He is really quite absurd.'

Adapted from a book about Mussolini, written by Christopher Hibbert in 1962. Lord Curzon was British Foreign Secretary from 1922 to 1924.

Exercise 6.4

Read **Section C** and **Source 6e**. Answer the questions in sentences.

a When did Mussolini come to power in Italy?
b What did Mussolini call himself?
c In which two ways was Mussolini like Stalin?
d What did Mussolini do to his enemies?
e 'The first ten years of his rule' (in **Source 6e**) means which ten-year period?
f Which facts about Mussolini's appearance can you find in **Source 6e**?
g What was Lord Curzon's opinion of Mussolini?

Prime Minister Tojo of Japan with his cabinet

7 Nazi Germany

Adolf Hitler at a Nazi rally in Dortmund in 1933

A The rise of the Nazis

Adolf Hitler was born in Austria. In the First World War, though, he served in the **German** army. (He fought bravely, but rose no higher than corporal.) When the war ended, he stayed in Germany and took to politics. He found that he had a gift for speaking — he could charm a crowd with his words. He was soon leader of his party, the National Socialists or **Nazis**.

Nazis hated the 'unfair' Treaty of 1919. They said that the statesmen who made peace had 'stabbed the German army in the back'. The Nazis were ready to risk war to change the Treaty. They wanted Germany to be a great power again. And they said it would be great when there was a one-party Nazi state, with Hitler as 'Führer' or dictator.

The Nazis made one attempt, in 1923, to seize power by force. This failed, and Hitler went to prison for a while. After that, they took part in elections. They won the votes of those who were ashamed of Germany's defeat, and people who hated the **Jews**. (Nazis blamed Jews for all that was wrong in Germany.) At the same time, their private army of young thugs fought with their rivals and spread fear in the streets.

But the Wall Street Crash of 1929 was the main cause of the Nazis' rise to power. As more people lost their jobs, the Nazis won more votes. By 1932, they were the biggest party in the German Parliament. Now, the leaders of the other parties needed the help of the Nazi votes. So they got the President to make Hitler **Chancellor** (Prime Minister). They thought that it would be easy to make the Austrian corporal do as they wished.

Now try Exercises 7.1 and 7.2.

Exercise 7.1

Read **Section A**, then copy out the sentences and fill in the missing words.

a Adolf Hitler was born in _____

b Hitler was a _____ in the German army in the First World War.

c The short name for the National Socialists was the _____

d The Nazis accused the German statesmen who made peace in 1918 of 'stabbing the German army _____ _____ _____ .

e The Nazis wanted Hitler to be Germany's _____

f The Nazis _____ Jews.

g The Nazis got more votes when _____ rose in Germany.

Exercise 7.2

Read the note on 'Causes' on page 20 again.

What were the **causes** of the Nazis' rise to power? Study **Section A**, then decide which points in the list below were reasons for Hitler's rise to the top. Write out the points which you think **were** causes of the Nazis' rise.

a Hitler was a skilful public speaker.
b The Germans disliked the Treaty of Versailles.
c Germans blamed the army for losing the war.
d Some Germans shared Hitler's views about Jews.
e The Nazis seized power by force.
f The Nazi private army beat up their opponents.
g The Wall Street Crash led to a big rise in unemployment.
h The leaders of the other parties were afraid of Hitler.
i The leaders of the other parties needed the help of the Nazis.

Inside the Reichstag (the German Parliament) in 1930. You can see the Nazi members, in their brown shirts, in the background.

B The Nazi dictatorship

Hitler soon showed how wrong the politicians were. In less than six months, Germany became a **one-party state**. The other parties either closed down, or they were banned. Hitler became the 'Führer', or dictator. He and his friends now had the power to do as they wished. They could change the laws, put people in prison, or make the Germans march to war.

The **Gestapo** and **S.S.** (state police) got rid of those who objected to Nazi rule. They rounded up the top men in the anti-Nazi parties and trade unions, and put them in **concentration camps**.

Nazi Germany

Spies were soon at work in factories, shops, clubs, and in each street. People who grumbled about the Nazis were sent to the camps.

It was the job of **Joseph Goebbels**, the Minister of **Propaganda**, to keep the people on the Nazis' side. So Goebbels took control of the press and radio. He made them give out the Nazi version of the news, and urge the Germans to love the Führer and hate the Jews. The 'wireless' brought Hitler's voice into every German home.

The Nazis tried to make sure that the children were on their side too. Schools taught young people to obey the Führer. New history textbooks told of the great deeds of the Germans of the past, and told lies about the 'wicked' Jews. New biology books 'proved' that the Germans were the **master race**. Teachers who would not swear to follow Hitler were sacked.

Now try Exercise 7.3.

A fundraising poster for the Hitler Youth

Early SS men carrying their standard. They began as Hitler's private bodyguard.

Exercise 7.3

Read **Section B** and **Sources 7a** and **7b**, and look at **Source 7c**.
How do the two written sources (**7a** and **7b**) differ in what they say about the Reichstag fire?

a Write a paragraph, saying what you think are the main differences between the accounts in **Sources 7a** and **7b**.

b Draw two cartoons, with pin-men if you like. One cartoon should show something that you can find in **Source 7a**. The other cartoon should show something that you can find in **Source 7b**.

Source 7a

On the night of 27 February (1933), the Reichstag building caught fire. The man who lit the fire was a half-mad Dutchman called van der Lubbe. The Nazis put the blame on the Communists. Four thousand Communists were arrested, and their newspapers were banned.

Adapted from a book written by Hermann Mau and Helmut Krausnich in 1959.

Source 7c   The Reichstag building on fire in February 1933

Source 7b

The Reichstag fire was planned by Goebbels. And the men who carried it out were under Goering's orders. An underground passage led from Goering's house to the Reichstag, which was close-by. And through this tunnel, one Karl Ernst led a small party of stormtroopers. They spread the chemicals and petrol, and lit the blaze. A few days before, the police had arrested a Dutch half-wit called van der Lubbe. They had overheard him boasting that he would set the Reichstag on fire.

Adapted from a book written by Robert Goldston in 1967.

C Jobs, guns, and Jews

The Nazis' biggest success was in finding work for the **unemployed**. Thousands of men were employed building the new motorways. Thousands more got jobs as civil service clerks. (A lot of them took the places of Jews who had been sacked.) And when the Nazis urged married women to stay at home, men took their posts in offices and schools.

But the main boost to jobs came when Hitler began to build up the army, navy, and air force again. From 1935, all young men had to do two years' **army service**. Large numbers of men got jobs in factories making tanks, guns, and planes. The shipyards were busy again, also, making warships and submarines.

All of this was good news for the owners of factories and shipyards. They made big profits from the arms orders, and were on good terms with Hitler and the Nazis. So were the officers in the armed forces. They were glad to see Germany strong and well-armed again. And most of them were ready to use these arms in war.

The people with least reason to like the Nazis, of course, were the Jews. When the Nazis came to power, Jewish teachers and civil servants were sacked. Books by Jewish authors were burned, and in 1935 a new law banned marriage between Christians and Jews. After 1938, Jews were not allowed to be doctors, lawyers, or businessmen. They could not go to cinemas or hotels, and they were not allowed to own cars. Rightly fearing that there might be worse to come, many Jews fled abroad.

Now try Exercise 7.4.

Source 7d

A Nazi stormtrooper stands outside a closed Jewish shop in 1933. His placard says 'Germans defend yourselves! Do not buy from Jews!'

Source 7e

One day in November 1938 ... I cycled into town. Along the main street, the windows of Jewish shops had been smashed. Their contents had been looted, and were lying torn, broken up and scattered. Shop signs with Jewish names had been hauled down. Books were burning outside a bookshop, and anti-Jewish slogans were screaming from walls and hoardings next to giant swastikas. Stormtroopers were in command of the street, and still more were arriving in open trucks.

Adapted from a book written by Marianne Mackinnon in 1987.

Source 7f

The Nazis encouraged Germans to hate the Jews. A lot of synagogues (Jewish temples) and shops owned by Jews were burned down. The fire brigade sometimes turned up, but it did not hurry. This is the remains of a synagogue in Berlin in November 1938.

Exercise 7.4

Read **Section C** and **Source 7e**, and look at **Sources 7d** and **7f**.
Write your own notes about the sources. They should answer these questions:

a How did the Nazis harm Jewish shopkeepers? (Find at least five things that they did.)
b Which Nazis did most of the burning, looting, etc.?
c What happened to synagogues in Nazi Germany? Why?
d Why do you think the fire brigade was told not to hurry?

8 The Origins of the Second World War

A Hitler and the Treaty of Versailles

In his book *Mein Kampf* ('My Struggle'), Hitler told the world that he wanted to change the 'unfair' Treaty of Versailles. (Look back to **Chapter 5, Section C**.) He also announced that Germany must have '**living space**' in Poland and Russia. And soon after he came to power, he resigned from the League of Nations, and began to rearm. (See **Chapter 7**.)

As early as 1933, people could see that Hitler's plans might lead to war. And if he was to be stopped, only the French and British were strong enough to do it. But the French had no plans to defend the states of eastern Europe. The French relied in the 1930s on a string of massive forts and trenches (the '**Maginot Line**') along their eastern border. It was there to defend France, not Poland or Russia.

The British wanted peace as much as the French did. The government spent as little as it could on arms. In any case, by the 1930s, the British had begun to think that parts of the Treaty of Versailles *were* unfair.

In Russia, Stalin was worried when Hitler came to power. In 1935 he signed a treaty with the French. But the British did not trust Stalin, and they said that although the Russian army was large, it was weak. So instead of standing up to Hitler, the British tried giving in — in 1935 they agreed to let him build **submarines** again. (The Treaty of Versailles said that the German navy could have no submarines.)

Now try Exercise 8.1.

Above left: British troops help to man a French Maginot Line fort in November 1939

Above right: A French recruitment poster using the Maginot Line

Exercise 8.1

Read **Section A**, then answer the questions.

a What was the title of Hitler's book?
b When was the Treaty of Versailles signed?
c Where did Hitler want 'living space' for Germany?
d Which were the only states strong enough to stand up to Hitler?
e What was the name of the system of forts on France's eastern border?
f When did the Russians and French sign a treaty?
g In 1935 the British agreed to let Hitler build what?

B Appeasement

The League of Nations was meant to keep the peace, but it failed its biggest tests. In 1935, Mussolini invaded **Abyssinia**. The League condemned him, and ordered members not to sell arms to Italy. But it did not stop the trade in oil. By the middle of 1936, the conquest was complete.

Hitler admired what Mussolini had done. So he too defied the League, and broke the Treaty of Versailles, when he sent German troops into the **Rhineland** in March 1936. The French and British did not fire a shot. It seemed that the dictators could do as they wished. They promised to keep out of the civil war which broke out in Spain in July 1936. But they broke their word, and sent help to **General Franco**, Spain's would-be dictator.

Neville Chamberlain, Britain's Prime Minister from 1937 to 1940, hated the thought of another war. So he tried what has been called 'appeasement'. It meant talking to the dictators, and giving them most of what they asked for. It kept the peace for a while, but in the end it led to war.

In 1938, Hitler showed that he meant to have more land for Germany in Europe. In March of that year, he sent his troops into **Austria**, and made it part of Germany. Chamberlain protested, but Hitler took no notice. (Most Austrians seemed quite pleased.)

In the summer of 1938, Hitler demanded the Sudetenland, the German part of **Czechoslovakia**. (Look at the map.) Then he threatened war if the Czechs did not give way. It seemed that there would be war, with Britain and France on the side of the Czechs. But in a meeting on 29 September in **Munich**, Chamberlain and the French agreed to make the Czechs give their land away.

Now try Exercise 8.2.

The Treaty of Versailles said that the German army could have no tanks. So they practised with dummies made out of wood and canvas!

Can we believe the sources?

You need to be careful with sources. The authors of books might not have known all the facts. Some authors tell the story to suit their own side. People say, 'The camera can't lie.' But photographs do not always tell the whole truth. And there are many questions that photographs can't answer.

Source 8a

German troops march into the Rhineland in 1936

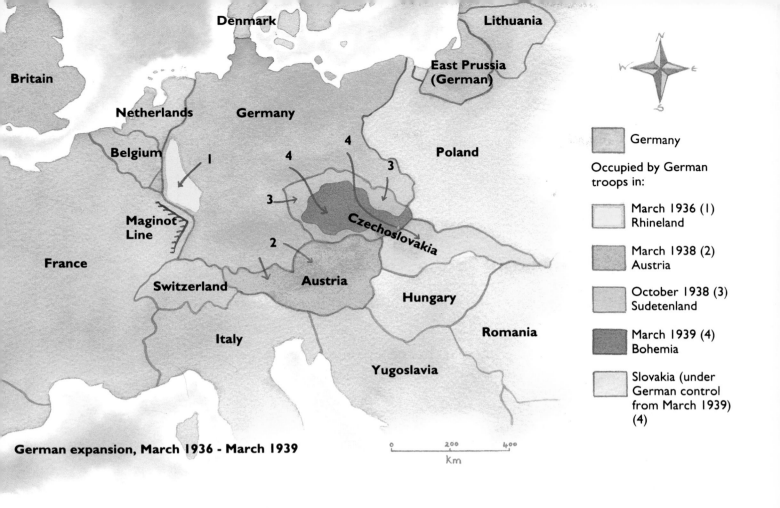

Germany

Occupied by German troops in:

March 1936 (1) Rhineland

March 1938 (2) Austria

October 1938 (3) Sudetenland

March 1939 (4) Bohemia

Slovakia (under German control from March 1939) (4)

German expansion, March 1936 - March 1939

0   200   400
km

Source 8b

Hitler enters Austria in 1938

Source 8c

The German army moved into the Sudetenland (the German part of Czechoslovakia) in October 1938

45

Exercise 8.2

Read **Section B**, and look at **Sources 8a, 8b** and **8c**.

a Copy the chart below and complete the blank spaces.

Source	Date	Where is it?	Primary or secondary source?	Do the people seem pleased?
8a	_____	_____	_____	_____
8b	_____	_____	_____	_____
8c	_____	_____	_____	_____

b Read the note 'Can we believe the sources?' Then answer this question: Do these photographs prove that **all** the people were happy with Hitler? (Write at least one sentence.)

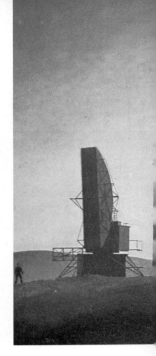

A radar station built on the south coast of England

C The outbreak of war

War was very close in the autumn of 1938. Men dug trenches in the London parks, **gas masks** were given out, and plans were drawn up to **evacuate** children (send them out of the towns to country areas). Experts were sure that if war came the cities would be bombed. And most of them thought that poison gas would be used.

Then the Munich meeting seemed to preserve peace. Hitler promised not to go to war with Britain. For a while, Chamberlain was a hero. But the British took no chances — factories worked hard making fighter planes, and **radar** stations were built along the south and east coasts. And from April 1939, all young men had to do six months' service in the forces.

Hitler had not given up his plans for eastern Europe. In March 1939, he swallowed up the rest of Czechoslovakia. Next, he began to demand the western part of **Poland**. Chamberlain could see now that appeasement had failed. In April 1939, he promised to help Poland if the Germans attacked.

Britain and France tried, and failed, to get **Russia** on their side. But Stalin signed a treaty with Hitler. Hitler swore that he would not attack Russia, and promised the Russians the eastern half of Poland. Now Hitler was ready — he knew that he would not have to fight the Russians as well as the Poles. On 1 September 1939, German troops invaded Poland. Two days later, Britain and France declared **war** on Germany.

Now try Exercises 8.3 and 8.4.

Source 8d

In May 1939, Hitler talked not only of war with Poland, but of war with the western powers (Britain and France) as well. He may have meant to go to war with Poland, but he did not want war with the western powers. He expected the nerve of the British and French to break. And he expected that they would force the Poles to give in. But it did not much matter to him whether the Poles fought or not, so long as they were alone.

Adapted from a book written by A. J. P. Taylor in 1961.

Exercise 8.3

Read **Section C**, and look back at **Section B**.

a Find out when these events happened. Write them out, with dates, in the correct order (earliest first).
   i Hitler sent German troops into Austria.
   ii Britain and France went to war with Germany.
   iii Hitler demanded the German part of Czechoslovakia.
   iv Hitler took over the rest of Czechoslovakia.
   v Italy invaded Abyssinia.
   vi The Munich conference took place.
   vii Chamberlain promised British help for Poland.
   viii Hitler sent German troops into the Rhineland.
   ix The German army invaded Poland.

b Draw a set of cartoons (three or four pictures, with pin-men if you wish) to show some of the events in this list.

Exercise 8.4

Read **Sources 8d** and **8e**, and the note 'Experts disagree', then discuss the questions in a group. Either report to the rest of the class what your group thinks, or make a tape.

a According to **Source 8e**,
   i Did Hitler want war with Poland?
   ii In April 1939, did Hitler expect that he would have to go to war with Britain and France?
   iii After Britain and France's promise to Poland, Hitler asked himself what question?
   iv Did Hitler think that he might have to fight Britain and France?

b According to **Source 8d**,
   i Did Hitler want war with Poland?
   ii Did Hitler want war with Britain and France?
   iii What did Hitler expect Britain and France to do?

A cartoon about Hitler's treaty with Stalin in 1939. It is shown as a three-legged race.

Experts disagree

Source **8e**

As early as April 1939, Hitler decided to smash Poland. At that time, he was sure that Britain and France would do nothing to help the Poles. When they promised to come to Poland's aid, Hitler hesitated. Should he attack first in the east or in the west? In the end, he decided that Poland would be the German army's first victim.

Adapted from a book written by Henri Michel in 1975.

Experts who study and write about history are called **historians**. They find out what happened in the past. And they try to work out **why** events happened as they did – what were their **causes**.

These experts do not always agree with each other. When they do not, we must look carefully at what they say, and try to spot the differences.

9 'Their Finest Hour'

A The conquest of Poland

Poland was the first victim of *Blitzkrieg* ('lightning war'). In the first two days of war, German fighters and dive-bombers destroyed most of the Polish air force on the ground. They bombed and strafed roads, railways, and bridges. Massed tanks (*panzers*) broke through the Polish lines. German infantry sped forward in lorries.

The speed and force of the German attack left the Poles trapped and confused. They fought bravely — more than once, their **cavalry** charged the German tanks. But they had no chance, and in a month they were beaten. Hitler took control of western Poland, and let Stalin have the east. To Hitler, the war was over, and he offered peace to Britain and France.

The allies did not make peace, but they did nothing to help the Poles. The French army manned the forts and blockhouses of their Maginot Line. British troops moved to the borders of France and Belgium, waiting for a German attack. They waited all through the winter of 1939–40, but no

attack came. Allied planes flew over German cities, and dropped leaflets, not bombs. Americans called it the **'Phoney War'**.

Then, on 9 April 1940, the Germans attacked **Denmark** and **Norway**. The Danes gave in straight away, but the king of Norway and his army resisted. The British and French sent help, but too little and too late. News of the defeats in Norway led to angry scenes in the House of Commons in London. Neville Chamberlain was forced to resign as Prime Minister, and on 10 May **Winston Churchill** took his place.

Now try Exercise 9.1.

Above left: The Norwegians fought bravely. Here you can see a German tank and some infantry forcing their way forward in central Norway in 1940.

Exercise 9.1

Read **Section A**. Write sentences to show that you know what these words mean:

blitzkrieg   dive-bomber   panzer   cavalry

blockhouse   leaflet   resist   resign

B The fall of France

Suddenly, on 10 May, the Germans attacked in the west. *Blitzkrieg* was turned on **Holland** and **Belgium**. Rotterdam was almost wiped out in a huge air-raid. Tanks roared through the Dutch and Belgian lanes and streets, while fighters and dive-bombers screamed above. After five days, the Dutch surrendered, and on 28 May the king of Belgium asked for peace.

Meanwhile, the panzers were storming through the Ardennes forest and into north-east **France**. On 20 May, they reached the coast at Abbeville. (Look at the map.) The allied armies were cut in two — the British and some of the French to the north, and the rest of the French to the south.

It seemed certain that the British army would be surrounded and destroyed. It retreated to Dunkirk, where ships of the Royal Navy, helped by a fleet of Channel steamers, fishing boats, barges and yachts, began to ferry the men home to England. Pounded by German aircraft and guns, the soldiers waited their turn on the beaches. By 3 June, **300,000** had been rescued. The army had lost its tanks, heavy guns and lorries, but most of its men had been saved.

Now the panzers swept south, then east. The Maginot Line was no use when attacked from the west. **Marshal Pétain**, a hero of the First World War, came to power in France, and made peace with the Germans on 22 June. The German army had won a great victory, and the German people went wild with delight. Hitler expected that Britain too would soon make peace.

Now try Exercises 9.2. and 9.3.

Polish cavalry training before the German invasion

German conquests, August 1939 - June 1940

Norway
Finland
Sweden
Denmark
Estonia
Latvia
Lithuania
U.S.S.R. (Russia)
Britain
Netherlands
Dunkirk
Abbeville
Belgium
Germany
Poland
Paris
France
Slovakia
Vichy
Switzerland
Hungary
Italy
Romania
Yugoslavia

⬛	Controlled by Germany in August 1939
⬜	Taken over by Germany in September 1939
⬛	At war with Germany from September 1939
⬛	Neutral states attacked by Germany in 1940
⬛	Neutral states
←	German invasions
⬜ Italy / ⬛ Russia	States friendly with Germany in 1939-1940
⬜	Taken over by Russia in September 1939
⬛	Taken over by Russia in 1940
⋯	After June 1940, border between occupied France and unoccupied France
↙	British evacuation from Dunkirk, May-June 1940

Exercise 9.2

Read **Section B**. Find the dates of the events below from **Section B** and the last paragraph of **Section A**. Write out the events, with their dates, in the correct order (earliest first).

a The end of the Dunkirk evacuation.
b The Germans attacked Holland and Belgium.
c The Belgians surrendered.
d The Germans attacked Denmark and Norway.
e The Dutch surrendered.
f The French surrendered.
g Winston Churchill became British Prime Minister.
h The German army reached Abbeville.

Source **9a**

> *The Battle of France is over. I expect that the Battle of Britain is about to begin. . . . Hitler knows that he will have to break us in this island or lose the war. If we stand up to him, all Europe may be free. . . . Let us therefore brace ourselves to our duties, so that if the British Empire lasts for a thousand years, men will still say: 'This was their finest hour.'*

Adapted from a speech made by Winston Churchill on 18 June 1940.

Source **9b** A British soldier tries to shoot down a German aircraft with a rifle at Dunkirk

Source **9c** On 22 June 1940, the French general, Bergeret, (right) signed the surrender of the French forces. The surrender took place in the same railway carriage in which the Germans had signed *their* surrender in 1918.

A British newspaper reports the Dunkirk evacuation

French refugees fleeing from the fighting in 1940

C The Battle of Britain

A Spitfire (front) and a Hurricane (behind) in flight

When Churchill did not ask for peace, Hitler began to make plans to invade Britain. His problem was the **English Channel** and the **Royal Navy**. (The British had a far stronger navy than the Germans.) Hitler saw that the answer lay in the **air**. If his air force could wipe out the R.A.F., it would be able to sink enough British warships to let an invasion fleet cross the Channel.

In August and September 1940, waves of German bombers and fighters attacked the airfields and ports of south-east England. The **Spitfires** and **Hurricanes** of R.A.F. Fighter Command 'scrambled' to meet them. (Thanks to **radar**, the R.A.F. knew how many Germans were coming, where, and when.) Men and women in the fields of Kent and Sussex watched the deadly 'dog-fights' in the skies above them.

The battle was fought by a few hundred young pilots. They had to be brave, skilful, and quick. Over 400 were killed on the allied side, and rather more Germans. Many others were shot down and rescued, often badly burned. Winston Churchill said, 'Never in the field of human conflict was so much owed by so many to so few.' By the '**few**' he meant the British pilots.

If the Germans had kept on bombing the airfields, they might have won the Battle of Britain. But in September they switched their attack and began bombing **London**. (See Chapter 15). The switch saved the R.A.F.'s airfields, and the fighters kept flying. So the Germans did not win command of the air, and Hitler had to give up his plan to invade Britain.

Now try Exercises 9.4 and 9.5.

Exercise 9.4

Read **Section C**, then answer the questions.

a Why could the Germans not invade Britain at once?
b If the Germans had defeated the R.A.F., what could their planes have done?
c What did the German air force attack first in August 1940?
d What were Spitfires and Hurricanes?
e Why was radar important to the R.A.F.?
f Who were 'the few'?
g What mistake did the Germans make in September 1940?
h Who won the Battle of Britain, and what was the result?
Draw a picture of a Spitfire or a Hurricane.

Exercise 9.5

Read **Sources 9d** and **9e**, and the note on 'taking sides'. Then write three short paragraphs about:

a What the sources tell you about the events at the end of August, 1940.
b What the British thought about the bombing of Berlin.
c What the Germans thought about the bombing of Berlin.

Source 9d

We answered the German air-raids on London at the end of August (1940) with an attack on Berlin. Because of the distance our bombers had to fly, it could only be on a small scale. But the War Cabinet were in a mood to hit back, and defy the Germans. I was sure that they were right.

Adapted from the *War Memoirs* which Winston Churchill wrote after 1945.

Source 9e

The R.A.F. came over again on the night of 28–29 August. Goebbels had let the papers print just a few lines on the first air-raid. Now he told them to cry out against the 'brutal' British flyers. They were attacking the defenceless women and children of Berlin, he said. Most of the papers carried the same headline: 'COWARDLY BRITISH ATTACK'. Two nights later, after the third raid, they read: 'BRITISH AIR PIRATES OVER BERLIN'.

Adapted from a book written by William Shirer in 1959.

Taking Sides

People often take sides – they are for one party, or they support one team. Men and women in the past took sides as well. In war-time, everyone took sides – what their own side did was right, and what their enemies did was wrong. It is useful to remember this when reading war-time sources.

10 The Russian Front, 1941-1943

Map legend:
- Controlled by Germany in June 1941
- Germany's allies in 1941
- Russian land conquered by the Germans, 1941-1942
- Neutral countries
- Britain } At war with Germany
- Russia }
- The Russian Pincer Attack at Stalingrad
- Allied convoy route to Russia

0   200   400 Km

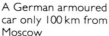

A German armoured car only 100 km from Moscow

A The German invasion of Russia

Even if he could not invade Britain, Hitler knew that the British alone could not beat him. Early in 1941, he thought that he was free to carry out his great plan of conquest in the east. This meant war with **Russia**, and the biggest *Blitzkrieg* of them all. By the middle of 1941, the Germans had three million men on their eastern front.

War with Russia meant breaking his treaty with Stalin. But breaking his word did not worry Hitler. What did worry him, though, was that his ally, Mussolini, needed help. Italy had attacked Greece, and was losing. So German armies were rushed to the

Balkans in the spring of 1941, and they quickly beat the Yugoslavs and Greeks. But this fighting in the Balkans delayed the attack on Russia by a month.

On 22 June 1941, the guns opened up on the eastern front. To the Russians, war came as a complete surprise. German planes bombed their air force as it stood on the ground. The panzers cut great holes in their front. Russian soldiers in their thousands were marched off as prisoners of war. In five months, the Germans advanced almost to the gates of **Moscow** and **Leningrad**. (Look at the map.)

But all was not well for the Germans. Their losses in dead and wounded were high. The autumn rain made a sea of mud, in which tanks and lorries sank and stuck. Autumn turned to winter, and the Germans were not dressed to keep out the Russian cold. And the Russian 'scorched earth' policy meant that as they retreated, the Russians wrecked their own railways, bridges and dams, and left no food, or coal, or oil.

Now try Exercises 10.1 and 10.2.

Motives

'What were the **motives** of the people of the past?' means 'What were their **reasons** for their actions?' or 'What did they hope to gain?'.
Some men and women have left sources telling us what their motives were. The sources do not always say the same, but that does not make some of them wrong. It is common for people to have more than one motive.

German armoured vehicles advancing through a Russian town. The German flags on the top of the tanks helped German aircraft to recognise their own men.

Exercise 10.1

Read **Section A**, **Sources 10a**, **10b** and **10c**, and the note on 'Motives'. What were Hitler's **motives** when he invaded Russia? Choose six motives from the list below, and write them out.

a To help win the war against Britain.
b To grow food for Germans.
c To make the Russians better off.
d To destroy Communism.
e To get more land for Germany.
f To employ the German army.
g To capture Russian slave-workers.
h To damage the Jews.
i To make the Germans masters of Europe.
j To test his latest weapons.

Exercise 10.2

Read the note 'Who wrote the sources?' Copy out the sentences, and write either TRUE or FALSE after each of them.

a **Source 10a** is taken from a book written by Hitler.
b **Source 10a** is a primary source.
c **Source 10b** was written by a Russian general.
d **Source 10b** is a secondary source.
e **Source 10c** is a primary source.
f Hitler always told the truth, and he never changed his mind.
g **Source 10a** was written just before Germany invaded Russia.
h What **Sources 10a**, **10b** and **10c** say may be true, but it could be partly false.

Who wrote the sources?

You have to ask questions about the people who wrote the sources. For example, was the author present at the time? Did the author know how things really were? Even a primary source may not tell us the truth. It may have been written many years before or after the event. Or its author may have told lies.

Source 10a

Germany must stop looking towards the south and west of Europe and turn to the east. When we speak of new land in Europe, we must think mainly of Russia and the states on her borders. This huge empire is ready to fall. When the Jews lose control of Russia, the state will soon collapse.

From Hitler's book, *Mein Kampf* ('My Struggle'), which he wrote in 1925.

Source 10b

Our main task is to see that the German people are fed. So the southern part of Russia will do the job of growing the food that the Germans need. We see no reason to feed the Russians with the food grown in southern Russia. The future will be very hard for the Russians.

Words spoken by Alfred Rosenberg, one of the Nazi leaders, in June 1941.

Source 10c

If Russia is smashed, Britain's last hope will be shattered. Then Germany will be the master of Europe. Therefore, Russia must be wiped out in the spring of 1941. The sooner Russia is smashed, the better.

Adapted from a speech made by Hitler to his generals in July 1940.

Source 10d

Men and women helped to defend Moscow. Here you can see an anti-tank ditch being dug by hand outside Moscow in 1941.

Source 10e

The Russian winter slowed the progress of the German army. Snow blocked roads and railways, so it was difficult to move soldiers and send them supplies of arms, food, and petrol.

B Russian resistance

Hitler had hoped to defeat Russia before the winter of 1941 set in. Some experts believe that he might have done so if the start of his war with Russia had not been delayed. (See **Section A**.) Others think that in the end the Germans were bound to lose. They say that Russia was too vast and her population was too large for Germany to conquer.

The farther the Germans advanced, the harder the Russians fought. Just before Christmas 1941, the Germans pressed hard to capture Moscow. But workers came out from the factories and joined the soldiers on the edge of the city. Then the Russian tanks **counter-attacked**, and drove the Germans back. It was the German army's first defeat since 1939.

Stalin urged everyone to work and fight for Russia in the '**Great Patriotic War**'. And the Russians did all they could — men, women, and children. Soldiers and airmen fought bravely at the front. '**Partisans**' blew up trains behind the German lines. Men and women worked flat out in the factories. None gave more than the people of **Leningrad** (now renamed St. Petersburg), who were bombed and starved in a siege that lasted two and a half years.

Churchill was glad to have Stalin as an ally. And for the rest of the war, Britain and the U.S.A. sent Russia huge amounts of arms. (See Chapter 13.) Stalin took the arms, but he was never grateful. He kept asking his allies to start a '**second front**' — launch an invasion of France. A 'second front' would force Hitler to move German troops from Russia to the west.

Now try Exercise 10.3.

> ## Exercise 10.3
>
> Read **Section B**, and study **Sources 10d, 10e, 10f** and **10g**. Why did the Germans not win a quick victory in Russia? What were the **causes** of their failure?
>
> **a** Write notes, giving a list of causes. (Use the last paragraph of **Section A**, **Section B**, and **Sources 10d, 10e, 10f** and **10g**.)
> **b** Describe what you can see in one of the photographs. Write a paragraph.

Source 10f

The German soldiers did not have the warm clothes and boots they needed to keep out the Russian winter cold

Source 10g

This patriotic Russian poster from 1942 is encouraging greater war production

СОРЕВНУЙТЕСЬ НА ЛУЧШУЮ ПОМОЩЬ ФРОНТУ!

C Stalingrad

Hitler was annoyed with his generals for their failure to take Moscow. He took charge of the army himself, and said that there would be no more retreats. On his orders, the Germans began to advance again in the summer of 1942. This time, they headed south-west, towards **Stalingrad** (now called Volgograd).

The German advance came to a halt in the streets of Stalingrad in October 1942. Hitler poured more and more men into the city, and Stalin did the same. Then the Russians sprang their trap. Thousands of tanks broke through the German lines to the north and south of the city. Giant Russian **pincers** began to close round Stalingrad. The German commander could see that his men were being cut off, and asked Hitler to let him retreat. The Führer said there was to be no retreat, so the German troops were doomed.

The two Russian armies met 60 kilometres west of Stalingrad, then began to close the ring. A German army of **300,000 men** was trapped in the city. For two months, the pincers slowly closed. German losses — killed in action, died of wounds, and frozen to death — were appalling. The battle ended on 2 February 1943. Only 90,000 Germans were left alive.

The battle at Stalingrad was the **turning point** of the war in Russia. It proved that the Russians could beat the German invaders. It gave the Russian people more faith in themselves, and in Stalin their leader. And it showed for the first time that Hitler could make mistakes.

Now try Exercise 10.4.

Russian soldiers advancing through the ruins of Stalingrad

Exercise 10.4

Read **Section C**, and look at the map on page 53.

a Complete sentences 1 to 7 below by choosing groups of words from the list on the right. Write out the complete sentences.

1 When they reached the outskirts of Moscow, the Germans had ...
2 Stalingrad lies on the river ...
3 Allied convoys brought supplies of arms to ...
4 The Russians made a ring round ...
5 Hitler refused to allow ...
6 The battle of Stalingrad lasted ...
7 After the battle of Stalingrad ...

- Murmansk in the north of Russia.
- the German army at Stalingrad.
- the Russians knew that they could beat the Germans.
- Volga, south-east of Moscow.
- from October 1942 to February 1943.
- the German army to retreat.
- advanced about 1,000 kilometres.

b Draw a sketch-map of Russia. Mark Moscow, Leningrad, Stalingrad, Murmansk, and the limit of the German advance.

The Outbreak of War in the Far East

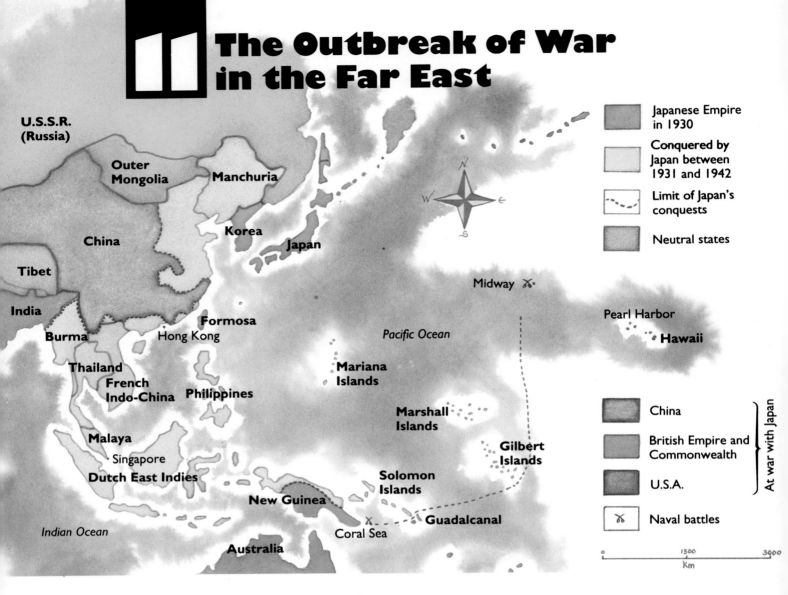

U.S.S.R. (Russia)

Outer Mongolia

Manchuria

Korea

Japan

China

Tibet

India

Burma

Formosa

Hong Kong

Thailand

French Indo-China

Philippines

Malaya

Singapore

Dutch East Indies

New Guinea

Indian Ocean

Australia

Midway

Pacific Ocean

Mariana Islands

Marshall Islands

Gilbert Islands

Solomon Islands

Guadalcanal

Coral Sea

Pearl Harbor

Hawaii

- Japanese Empire in 1930
- Conquered by Japan between 1931 and 1942
- Limit of Japan's conquests
- Neutral states
- China
- British Empire and Commonwealth — At war with Japan
- U.S.A.
- Naval battles

0   1500   3000
Km

Note:
Russia did not enter the war against Japan until August 1945

A The Japanese Empire

In the 1920s, Japan was the rising power of the Far East. She was the first country in Asia to have large-scale modern **industry**. Soon, her firms began to compete in the markets of the world. Critics said that the Japanese were good at copying the west, but had no ideas of their own. But the critics ignored the skill and hard work of Japan's people.

Japan grew rich enough to afford a large **army** and a modern **navy**. With her strong forces, she was able to conquer an empire, mainly at the expense of China. As well as the islands of Japan itself, she ruled Korea, Formosa, and part of northern China. (Look at the map.)

In 1931, the Japanese army in northern China seized control of the whole of **Manchuria**. China asked the League of Nations for help, and the League sent a team of experts to find out the facts. In the end, the League said that Japan was guilty of **aggression**. But it did nothing more. Even this was too much for the generals who were now in charge of Japan's government. In 1933, they resigned from the League.

By this time, Japan was firmly on the side of the **dictators**. (She signed a treaty with Germany in 1936.) In the next year, she began a full-scale war with China. Japan's army was on top, but the Chinese refused to give more land away. So the war went on, and by 1941 most of eastern China was in Japanese hands.

Now try Exercise 11.1.

Japanese soldiers in Manchuria in 1931

Exercise 11.1

Read **Section A**, and look at the map. Then fill in the missing words in the sentences. The words are given below, but not in the right order.

aggression	army	China
dictators	eastern	industry
Manchuria	navy	Formosa

a In Japan, _____ was more advanced than in other parts of Asia.

b Japan's _____ and _____ were bigger and more advanced than China's.

c Japan ruled the island of _____ off China's east coast.

d In 1931, Japan seized _____, which was part of northern China.

e The League of Nations said that Japan was guilty of _____

f By 1933, Japan was on the side of the _____ (Hitler and Mussolini).

g War between Japan and _____ began in 1937.

h By 1941, Japan controlled the _____ part of China.

B Pearl Harbor

The aim of **General Tojo**, the Minister of War, was to conquer a great empire for Japan. He wanted to take most of China, and south-east Asia too. If Japan could seize Malaya and the Dutch East Indies, she would have all the tin, rubber, and oil that she needed.

As a first step, Japanese troops moved into French Indo-China in July 1941. Churchill in Britain and **President Roosevelt** of the U.S.A. were both alarmed. They did not want to see any more conquests by Japan. So to punish her, they stopped all her foreign trade. (This meant cutting off her supplies of oil.) The risk of war was growing.

The **emperor** of Japan thought that his forces could never win a war with the U.S.A. So he was in favour of peace. But Tojo said that Japan should strike swift, hard blows against the U.S.A. and Britain. And while they were reeling, she should conquer the whole of south-east Asia. Then she could make peace, keeping most of the land that she had gained.

Tojo became Prime Minister in October 1941. On the morning of 7 December, aircraft from Japanese carriers bombed the U.S. fleet as it lay in its base at **Pearl Harbor** in Hawaii. Japan did not declare war, and gave no warning to the U.S.A.. Five battleships were sunk, and there was heavy loss of life.

Two days later, the shocked and angry members of the U.S. Congress voted for war with Japan. In less than a week, Britain was at war with Japan as well. And Hitler, true to his ally for once, declared war on the U.S.A.. So Britain and the United States were **allies** again at last.

Now try Exercises 11.2 and 11.3.

Source 11a

When we got the news of Pearl Harbor, there was bedlam. Sirens were going off, and aircraft guns firing. It was panic. There we were in the middle of the night, with no enemy in sight, but somebody thought they saw the enemy. They were shooting at random. All policemen were ordered to their stations, to await orders. No orders came, because there was no attack.

Adapted from the words of Tom Bradley, who was a young policeman in Los Angeles in 1941.

The Japanese attack on Pearl Harbor in Hawaii on 7 December 1941

Source 11b

I heard the news about Pearl Harbor on the radio. Though we had read in the paper that this sort of thing might happen, it still came as a shock. I was fourteen, in middle school. Both my parents, my two brothers, four sisters and I were living together. We were thrilled at first by the news of this victory. We weren't thinking about how it would turn out.

Adapted from the words of Akira Miuri, who lived in Tokyo in 1941.

Exercise 11.2

Read **Section B** and **Sources 11a**, **11b** and **11c**. Answer the following questions.

a Write down three things that happened in Los Angeles on the night of 7 December 1941.
b Why was there panic in Los Angeles?
c What was Tom Bradley's job?
d Where was Akira Miuri on 7 December 1941?
e How did Akira Miuri find out about the Japanese attack on Pearl Harbor?
f What were the thoughts of Akira Miuri and his family?
g Where was Peter Ota on 7 December 1941?
h Why do you think Peter Ota's father was arrested?
i What were Peter Ota's mother's feelings when she saw her husband?

Exercise 11.3

a Write a few sentences about Sources **11a**, **11b** and **11c**. Who spoke the words? (Are they primary or secondary sources? (Give a reason for your answer.)
b The sources are all about what people thought and did when they heard the news of Pearl Harbor. Which of these do the sources tell us about:
  i What Americans in Los Angeles thought about the news.
  ii What Americans in New York thought.
  iii What ordinary Japanese people in Tokyo thought.
  iv What the commanders of the Japanese army and navy were thinking.
  v What the president of the U.S.A. was thinking.
  vi What happened to Japanese-Americans.

Source 11c

On the evening of 7 December 1941, my father was at a wedding. He was dressed in a tuxedo. When the reception was over, F.B.I. agents rounded up at least a dozen guests, and took them to the county jail. For a few days, we heard nothing. When we found out where he was, my mother, my sister and I went to the jail. When my father walked into the lobby, my mother cried. He was in prison clothes, with a denim jacket and a number on his back.

Adapted from the words of Peter Ota, who lived in Los Angeles in 1941. His parents were Japanese.

C Japanese conquests

At the same time as Pearl Harbor, Japan bombed the U.S. fleet in the **Philippines**. With these two blows, she gravely weakened the U.S. navy in the **Pacific Ocean**. Tojo's ships could now land his men wherever he liked. In the first four months of 1942, Japan's forces spread south and eastwards through the islands of the Pacific. (Look at the map on page 58.)

A few days after Pearl Harbor, Japan's armies swept south from Indo-China to **Malaya**. In the South China Sea, her bombers sank two of Britain's biggest and best warships. On 15 February 1942, her troops took Britain's fortress of **Singapore**. No less than 60,000 men marched off as prisoners of war. By the end of June 1942, **Burma** and the **East Indies** had fallen too.

Why did the Japanese do so well? The fact that they took the allies by surprise is only part of the answer. Their aircraft were good and their pilots were skilful. They destroyed a lot of allied planes before they could take off. And the R.A.F., in any case, had no aircraft to spare for the Far East. Also, Japan's soldiers were tough and very brave. To them, it was an honour to die for Japan, and surrender meant shame.

The Japanese said that they were fighting to free the people of Asia from rule by the French, British, and Dutch. But the people did not get freedom. Instead, they got a Japanese reign of terror. Even worse was the treatment of the prisoners of war. Thousands of allied men were starved and worked to death in the jungle prison camps.

Now try Exercises 11.4 and 11.5.

Source **11d**

Singapore was Britain's main naval base in the Far East. Its big guns pointed out to sea, and could not be turned to face the land. But the Japanese attacked by land. They forced the British to surrender on 15 February 1942.

Exercise 11.4

Read **Section C** and look at **Source 11d**.
What were the **causes** of Japan's victories at the beginning of the war? Write notes in your own words, giving at least five reasons why the Japanese won so many battles and took so much land.

Exercise 11.5

Draw a sketch-map of the Far East and Pacific. Mark Japan, China, Korea, Manchuria, Hong Kong, the Philippines, Hawaii, Indo-China, Thailand, Malaya, Singapore, Dutch East Indies, New Guinea, Australia, Burma, India, Pacific Ocean, Indian Ocean. Draw arrows to show Japan's conquests, 1931–1942.

The main targets of the Japanese bombers at Pearl Harbor were the American aircraft carriers. However, none of the carriers were there when the Japanese attacked. The survival of the U.S. carriers was very important for the war in the Far East. (See Chapter 19.) This is the USS Lexington at the Gilbert Islands in 1943.

12 The War in North Africa and Italy

German-controlled by 1942

Italian

Germany's other allies by 1942

French

British

Neutral

→ German/Italian advances

← British/American advances

Italian soldiers watch the arrival of the Afrika Korps in the desert

A The threat to Egypt

Mussolini did not join Hitler's side in the war until 10 June 1940. This was just twelve days before France made peace. By then, it looked as though Britain would not last long either. Mussolini thought that the war would give him a chance to take more land for his empire. **Libya** was Italy's already, and he hoped to get **Tunisia** from France and capture **Egypt**, which was under British control. (Look at the map.)

Egypt would give him control of the **Suez Canal**, the main sea route from Europe to the east. So in September 1940 he sent his troops forward from

Libya into Egypt. They did not get far. The British gave ground at first, then, at the end of the year, they struck back. They won a crushing victory in the desert, took 100,000 prisoners, and advanced deep into Libya.

Hitler was not pleased with his ally. But in February 1941 he sent a German army, which the Germans called the *Afrika Korps*, to help him. Its commander, **Erwin Rommel**, was one of the best generals in the war. Even the British admired him – they called him the '**Desert Fox**'. The British Eighth Army called themselves the '**Desert Rats**'.

The War in North Africa and Italy

Rommel might have made great conquests if Hitler had sent him more men and arms. But Hitler did not do so — he needed them for the Russian front. Even so, Rommel went on the attack in June 1942. His army reached **El Alamein**, more than 200 miles inside Egypt. It looked certain to reach the Suez Canal, and give Hitler control of the whole Middle East.

Now try Exercises 12.1 and 12.2.

Exercise 12.1

Read **Section A** and look at the map on page 63. Write out the sentences and fill in the blank spaces.

a _____ lies to the east of Libya.

b _____ lies to the west of Libya.

c The main sea route to the east passed through the _____ Canal.

d Malta is an island in the _____ Sea.

e Algeria and Tunisia belonged to _____ in 1940.

f Sicily and Libya belonged to _____ in 1940.

g Malta and Egypt belonged to _____ in 1940.

Exercise 12.2

Read **Source 12a**. Answer the questions in two or three short paragraphs.

a Who wrote **Source 12a**?
b How do you know that **Source 12a** is a primary source?
c Which facts can you find in **Source 12a**?
d What were the soldier's opinions?

Source 12a

When we took Tobruk (in June 1942), the British rations fell into our hands. We were all impressed by how much food they had, and by how good it was. They had marvellous tinned fruit from their colonies. There were different kinds of jam, lots of corned beef, and meat and vegetable stew. Our rations were poor. And when they did not reach us, we had to make do with Italian army hard tack. This was tinned meat, with 'A.M.' stamped on it. We said it stood for 'Armer Mussolini' (poor Mussolini).

Adapted from a German soldier's account of the war in the desert.

German tanks advance past a captured British Bren gun carrier in the desert

B El Alamein and 'Operation Torch'

The further Rommel advanced, the further his supplies of arms, oil, and food had to come. All these supplies were brought to Libya by sea from Italy. So the ships had to sail past **Malta**, which was a British base. Aircraft and ships from Malta caused Rommel heavy losses. This was why, in 1941 and 1942, the Germans bombed Malta day and night.

Meanwhile, the British in Egypt had been getting more guns, planes, and tanks. Most of the ·new tanks were 'Shermans' from the U.S.A.. So the **Eighth Army** got stronger at a time when the 'Afrika Korps' was weaker. In July 1942, it fought and stopped the Germans at **El Alamein**. Three months later, it turned from defence to attack.

By then, the Eighth Army had a new commander, **Sir Bernard Montgomery** ('Monty' to his men). In a twelve-day battle at El Alamein in October, he destroyed more than half of Rommel's army. Then the Eighth Army's tanks rolled forward. In the next two weeks, they advanced 700 miles. Before long, the whole of Libya was in their hands.

The Eighth Army's advance was one half of an allied plan. The other half was '**Operation Torch**' — landings by **Americans** in Algeria in November 1942. 'Torch' went well, and the Americans advanced on Tunis. Here, they took Rommel's army from behind as it was forced westwards by the British. In May 1943, 250,000 Germans and Italians surrendered to the allies in Tunis. The war in North Africa was over.

Now try Exercises 12.3 and 12.4.

Malta during the 'blitz' – these are the ruins of the opera house

Exercise 12.3

Read **Section B**. Find the dates of these events in **Sections A** and **B**. Write out the events and dates in the correct order (earliest first):

a Hitler sent the 'Afrika Korps' to North Africa.
b The Germans and Italians surrendered in Tunis.
c Italy invaded Egypt.
d The 'Torch' landings took place in Algeria.
e The Battle of El Alamein.
f Italy entered the war.
g Rommel reached El Alamein.
h The British army in Egypt defeated the Italians.

Source 12b

Soldiers of the German 'Afrika Korps' pull a gun into position in the desert.

Source 12c

At 8.45 p.m. suddenly the entire enemy line burst into life. Soon it was one sheet of fire from end to end. The red flashes of exploding shells lit up our positions. The clear sky echoed with the thunder of the barrage, and it was filled with the blinding light of the flares. At the same time, bombs rained down on our gun-positions, tracks, tents and huts.

Adapted from an Italian officer's account of the Battle of El Alamein.

Source 12d

About 9 p.m. we moved forward and took up our positions on the start-line — a tape stretching across the desert. .... Suddenly the silence was broken by the crash of a single gun. The next moment a mighty roar split the air. The ground shook under us as salvo after salvo crashed out from hundreds of guns. Shells whined over our heads in a continuous stream. Soon we saw the enemy lit up by bright flashes.

Adapted from a British officer's account of the Battle of El Alamein.

Source 12e

A British armoured car in North Africa

Exercise 12.4

Read **Sources 12c** and **12d**, and look at **Sources 12b** and **12e**. Answer the questions in sentences.

a Which details are the same in **Sources 12c** and **12d**?
b Which sentence tells us that the author of **Source 12c** was being fired at?
c How do you know that the British guns fired from behind the front line?
d What do you think the 'start-line' was (**Source 12d**)?
e Why do you think the German soldiers in **Source 12b** are moving the gun?
f Why do you think it took so many soldiers to move the gun?
g What do you think the British soldiers in **Source 12e** are shooting at?

C Italy changes sides

Where should the allies strike at Hitler next? Stalin was certain that Britain and the U.S.A. should land troops in northern **France** and start what he called a 'second front'. (He thought that this would force Hitler to move some of his troops from the Russian front.) But Churchill was sure that the allies were still too weak in men and arms. He said that if they invaded France in 1943 they would be driven back into the sea.

Churchill persuaded Roosevelt to invade **Italy** first. He hoped that in a few weeks the allies could knock Italy out of the war. And he thought that Hitler's empire might then begin to collapse. He was only partly right. Italy was knocked out, but this was not the end for Hitler.

Sicily fell quickly to the allies in July 1943. Two months later, they invaded the mainland of Italy, and made good progress at first. These shocks caused big changes in Italy. The king dismissed Mussolini, and put him under arrest. The new government made peace with the allies, then entered the war again, this time on the *allied* side.

But Hitler did not give up Italy for lost. First, he sent **airborne troops** to carry out a daring rescue of Mussolini from his mountain prison. Then he strengthened the Germany army in Italy. The allies had to fight hard for each step forward. Losses in killed and wounded were high, and progress was slow. The allies took **Rome** in June 1944, but by that time their chief concern was France. (See Chapter 18.)

Now try Exercise 12.5.

'I suppose you realize you're driving on the wrong side of the road.'

Results

Causes come before events. **Results** come after events. One **result** of unemployment in Germany was that the Nazis got more votes. The **result** of El Alamein was that the British advanced from Egypt to Tunis.

Exercise 12.5

Read **Section C** and the note on 'Results'. Discuss these questions in a group. Either write out your answers or make a group tape.

a What did Stalin think would be the result if the allies invaded France?

b What did Churchill think would be the result if the allies tried to invade France in 1943?

c What did Churchill think would be the results if the allies invaded Italy?

d What were the results of the allied invasion of Sicily and Italy?

e In what way was Churchill wrong about the results of invading Italy?

13 The War at Sea and in the Air

A Starving the enemy out

As in the First World War, the Royal Navy imposed a blockade on the German ports. (See Chapter 3, Section C.) The British aim was to cut off vital supplies of food, oil, rubber, cotton, etc. from the Germans.

The blockade did close the German North Sea ports, but it did not bring the Germans to their knees. With the conquest of eastern Europe, the Germans got Polish and Russian grain, and Romanian oil. Neutral Sweden sold them iron ore. And German chemists found ways to make **artificial** rubber, textiles, and oil.

Britain relied on **imports** − more than half her food came from abroad. So, as in the First World War, the Germans tried to starve Britain into peace by sinking her ships. Their main weapon was the submarine, or **U-boat**, and its **torpedoes**. The U-boats began as soon as war broke out − they sank eleven British ships in the first week.

As well as U-boats, the Germans had some modern, well-armed surface ships. And if, after the fall of France in 1940, they had got hold of the **French navy**, they would have been stronger still. That is why the British asked the French fleet at Oran in North Africa to come over to their side. When the French refused, the British opened fire.

Now try Exercise 13.1.

German submarines (U-boats) at Kiel in north Germany

A recruitment poster for the German U-boat service in 1942

Ships of the Royal Navy shelled the French fleet at Oran in North Africa on 3 July 1940. They sank three battleships and killed 1300 French sailors.

Exercise 13.1

Read **Section A**. What were the aims of the British and Germans? Write at least one sentence in answer to each question.

a What were the aims of the British when they imposed a blockade on German ports?

b Why were Poland, Russia, and Romania useful to the Germans?

c Why did the Germans get their scientists to look for ways of making artificial oil, etc?

d What was the main aim of the German submarine campaign?

e Why did the British ask the French fleet to join their side?

f Why did the British fire on the French fleet at Oran?

Draw a picture of a submarine.

B The Battle of the Atlantic

Britain's answer to the U-boats was the same as in the First World War — **convoys**. Merchant ships had to sail in groups, guarded by **destroyers** of the Royal Navy. The main convoy route was across the **North Atlantic** from the U.S.A. And it was here that Americans first saw action. Their navy helped guard the convoys long before the U.S.A. entered the war.

The U-boats almost won the war for Hitler. They sank six million tons of **allied shipping** in 1942. At times, **foods stocks** in Britain ran very low. Between 1939 and 1945, 30,000 merchant seamen lost their lives. Thousands of others were **torpedoed** and then saved, some four or five times.

Convoys taking supplies of arms to Russia ran the biggest risks. The route lay close to the northern coast of Norway, which was in German hands. So the convoys were attacked by aircraft as well as U-boats, and sometimes more than half the ships were

Source 13a

A British convoy in the Atlantic

sunk. Losses were worst in the summer, when the sun never sets in the 'Land of the Midnight Sun'. In 1942 and 1943, the convoys had to be stopped for a while.

In the end, the allies won the Battle of the Atlantic. One reason was that the allied destroyers were fitted with **radar**. A second reason was that R.A.F. planes, in radio contact with the navy, patrolled the seas. As a result, the destroyers could find and destroy more U-boats. The Germans lost so many submarines that in 1943 they withdrew their whole fleet from the Atlantic. They kept up their attacks on the Russian convoys, though.

Now try Exercises 13.2 and 13.3.

A British convoy escort in Murmansk Harbour, in northern Russia

Exercise 13.2

Read **Section B**. Find words and phrases in **Section B** which mean the same as the groups of words below.

a The German name for submarines.
b A group of merchant ships sailing together for safety.
c Warships which guarded convoys.
d Ships belonging to Britain and the nations on Britain's side.
e Supplies of food in warehouses and shops.
f Sunk by an explosive underwater missile fired from a submarine.
g The part of Norway where the sun shines all night in mid-summer.
h A device using radio waves to spot aircraft, ships, etc.

Exercise 13.3

Read **Source 13b** and look at **Source 13a**. Write three short paragraphs answering these questions:

a What did a convoy look like? What could the man in **Source 13a** be looking for with his binoculars?
b In which two ways might convoys be attacked? Why was it safer to sail in a convoy than alone?
c Which was the most dangerous convoy route? Why was that route specially dangerous?

Source 13b

The third time I tried for Murmansk, I made it. It was early in 1945. Convoys were safer by then. We were using aircraft carriers and cruisers as well as destroyers (as escorts). Even so, we lost five or six ships. German pilots towards the end of the war were not so good. But it was still a deadly run.

Adapted from the words of David Milton, who was a sailor in the American merchant navy.

C **The war in the air**

The Germans bombed London every night from September to November 1940. Then they switched to the provinces, and kept up the attack until May 1941. After that, there were fewer raids, until the V1s began in 1944. (Chapter 15 describes the 'Blitz'.)

While the German raids on Britain grew less, the **R.A.F.**'s raids on Germany got bigger. And from 1942, the **U.S. Air Force**, flying from bases in England, joined in. News of big allied air attacks on Germany cheered the British people at a time when there was not much good news.

The British and Germans learned in 1940 that **daylight bombing** did not work — too many planes were shot down by fighters. So bombers had to fly by night. But at night, pilots could not find small targets, such as arms factories and bridges. That is why both sides switched to huge raids on whole cities. They hoped that some of the bombs would fall on key targets. They also hoped that civilians would lose the will to go on with the war.

But the Americans flew by day. Their **'flying fortresses'** were mighty bombers, with a lot of guns. From 1943 they flew with long-range fighter escorts, which drove off the German fighters. They aimed for smaller targets, such as single factories and arms dumps.

The R.A.F. and the U.S. Air Force pounded the German cities to rubble. But bombing did not make the Germans cry for peace. Until late in 1944, not much harm was done to industry. German factories were turning out more planes in 1944 than in 1940. But in the end, bombing did shorten the war. Allied bombers stopped the German trains from running, and destroyed so many oil stores that the Germans had no fuel for their tanks or planes.

Now try Exercise 13.4.

Lancaster bombers from 44 Squadron in 1942. From early 1942 the Lancaster was the R.A.F.'s main heavy bomber.

British Bombers now attack Germany a thousand at a time!

A poster showing the extent of the Allied bombing raids

Exercise 13.4

Read **Section C** and **Sources 13c** and **13d**. Discuss these questions in a group.

a Which source says that bombing was a success? Which source says that it was a failure?

b What are the main points in **Source 13c**? (Put them into your own words.)

c What reasons are there for thinking that the author of **Source 13c** would be right?

d What are the main points in **Source 13d**? (Put them into your own words.)

e What reasons are there for thinking that the author of **Source 13d** would be right?

f Is it possible that both sources are right about bombing?

Prepare a report for the rest of the class, saying what your answers are, or make a tape.

Source 13c

Bombing had far less effect than was thought at the time. The German arms industry increased its output until the autumn of 1944, in spite of the air-raids. The attacks on German ball-bearing plants almost grounded their air force for a while. But by the end of the war, they had more ball-bearings than they needed. Our attacks on the aircraft factories were a total failure. ...Bombing was meant to destroy German industry and the spirits of the people. It did neither.

Adapted from the words of Professor J. K. Galbraith, who toured Germany at the end of the war to find out how much damage bombing had done.

Source 13d

For the allies, bombing had some good results. Two million Germans had to be employed on repair work. German soldiers must have been depressed, thinking about their wives and children at home. Thousands of men who could have been at the front were manning anti-aircraft guns. Hundreds of fighter planes, instead of helping the army, had to defend the cities.

Adapted from a book written by Henri Michel in 1975. The author spent many years studying the Second World War.

'Flying Fortresses' of the U.S. Air Force on their way to bomb Stuttgart in July 1944

14 'Blood, Toil, Tears and Sweat'

Women making aircraft emergency dinghies in a factory

A Total war

The whole British nation was involved in war from 1939 to 1945. Women had to do war work. Children went through air-raids and put up with **food-rationing**. Men, of course, were affected first. An act passed in 1939 said that all men between 18 and 41 could be called up for service in the forces. And in 1940, after Dunkirk, men up to the age of 65 were allowed to volunteer for the **'Home Guard'**. More than a million did so.

Industry, of course, had to keep going. The army had to have guns, tanks, and shells. The factories that turned them out used steel and coal, so men were needed in the steel-works and coal-mines. Transport was vital, so men had to work on the railways and in the docks. Workers in these **'reserved occupations'** were not called up for the army.

In 1941, the government made war work compulsory for **unmarried women**. Some joined the forces. Women served as drivers and clerks, taking over from men who went off to fight. Many women worked in factories, making everything from uniforms to Spitfires. And the **'Land Girls'** took the place of farm workers who had gone to war.

The factories had to have metal as well as workers. When the government asked for scrap metal to make planes and tanks, people gladly gave their pots and pans. Miles of iron railings went into the furnaces. But Britain alone could not make all the arms her forces needed. Help came from the U.S.A., even before it entered the war. By 1944, half of Britain's tanks and two thirds of its transport planes came from America.

Now try Exercises 14.1 and 14.2.

Women launching a barrage balloon attached to steel cables. They forced enemy bombers to fly higher.

Exercise 14.1

Read **Section A**. Write out the sentences below, and add either TRUE or FALSE after each of them.

a From 1939, war work was compulsory for women.
b All men from 18 to 41 could be forced to join the army, navy, or R.A.F.
c The age-limit for the Home Guard was supposed to be 65.
d Some men who worked in coal-mines and steel-works were not called up.
e All dockers had to join the navy.
f No women were allowed to join the forces.
g People were asked to give up metal objects to help make more arms.

Exercise 14.2

Read **Sources 14a** and **14b**. Make notes in your own words, answering these questions:

a Which facts can you find in **both** sources?
b Which facts can you find only in **Source 14a**?
c Which facts can you find only in **Source 14b**?

Source 14a

Too many miners had joined the forces. The government now tried to get them back to the mines, but not enough came. Some young men had to be ordered to go into the mines, rather than into the forces. These 'Bevin Boys' did their best, and the coal crisis was avoided.

Adapted from a book written by T. O. Lloyd in 1970.

Source 14b

Late in 1943, the hated system of balloting for 'Bevin Boys' began. As young men came of age to join the forces, the ballot picked out one in ten. It was no use protesting that you wanted to fly jet fighters instead. Some boys refused and were jailed.

Adapted from a book written by Angus Calder in 1969.

B Rationing

One aim of the German U-boat campaign was to cut off Britain's food supplies. The government in Britain knew that food would be short, and brought in rationing at the start of the war. The Ministry of Food issued **ration books**, and decided how much meat, butter, bacon, etc. each person would get each week. No-one went hungry, but not many were overweight. In fact, experts say that rationing was good for the nation's health.

Source 14c

A Government poster urging farmers to grow as much food as possible

Some foods vanished from the shops. Bananas were not seen again until after the end of the war. Tomatoes and some fruit were very hard to get. And fish, which was never rationed, was greatly in demand. The result of rationing was that most housewives spent a large part of the war standing in **queues**.

The government tried to get as much food as possible grown at home. It encouraged farmers to plough up pasture and grow grain instead. It urged townspeople with back gardens to grow vegetables. **'Dig for Victory'** posters told them that they could beat Hitler by digging up their flower beds and lawns.

By 1941, **clothes** as well as food were rationed. Each person was allowed so many 'points' per year, and each clothes item was priced in points as well as money. So if you wanted a new coat, you had to save up your points. And you could not have a new pair of shoes as well. But if clothes were a problem, **petrol** was worse — there was none at all for private use. Car-owners locked their garage doors and waited for peace.

Now try Exercise 14.3.

Source 14d

A woman with her family's ration books. She has just bought her family's soap ration – one bar each. Every man, woman, and child had his or her own ration book.

Source 14e

you never know who's listening!

CARELESS TALK COSTS LIVES

A Government poster telling people to keep quiet about secret information

Exercise 14.3

Read **Section B**, and look at **Sources 14c**, **14d** and **14e**. Write three paragraphs to answer the questions below.

a Describe **Source 14c**. Why is the picture divided in two? What is the poster urging farmers to do? How did ploughing more land help to 'keep our ships and money free for buying vital arms'?

b Describe **Source 14d**. What can you tell about the woman's family? What do you think she is trying to work out?

c Describe **Source 14e**. Where do you think the two women are? Who are the two men sitting behind them? What is the poster suggesting? What is the poster trying to do?

C **Keeping spirits up**

Winston Churchill was a great war leader. He had one aim above all, and that was to win. To reach that goal, he worked day and night, and expected all who worked with him to do the same. Those who did not, and men who did not get results, were sacked. Churchill bullied his ministers, civil servants, and generals, and drove them to the limit and beyond.

The public knew Churchill from his speeches. At key moments in the war, he spoke on the radio (or '**wireless**' as it was then called). And the B.B.C. and newspapers passed on to the people what he said in the House of Commons. He told his listeners what they wanted to hear — that Britain would never give in. He stood for the '**Dunkirk spirit**' — the feeling that, even though Britain was alone, it would fight on until victory was won.

Churchill warned the people to expect a **German invasion** in 1940. So they got ready to resist. Soldiers who had no rifles drilled with broom handles. Men and women worked ten-hour shifts, seven days a week, in the arms factories. Old men in their seventies complained when they were not allowed to join the Home Guard.

The **B.B.C.** did a great deal to keep the nation's spirits up. Its news reports were thought to be honest and fair, so the people trusted what they heard. And it kept them entertained. It made them cry with the songs of **Vera Lynn** (the 'Forces' Sweetheart'), and it made them laugh with shows such as **I.T.M.A.** (The letters stood for 'It's That Man Again'. The 'man' was the show's star, Tommy Handley.)

Now try Exercises 14.4 and 14.5.

Vera Lynn 'The Forces' Sweetheart'

Exercise 14.4

Read **Section C** and **Sources 14f** and **14g**. Answer the questions in sentences.

a When and where did Winston Churchill make these speeches. (**Sources 14f** and **14g**)
b When he made the speeches, Churchill had just taken on which job?
c Are the speeches primary or secondary sources?
d Churchill said that his aim was what?
e Did Churchill think that it would be easy to win the war?
f Did he think that the Germans might invade Britain?
g What was he trying to encourage the people to do?
h What was he not prepared to do?

Members of the
Home Guard learning
how to use a sten gun

Source 14f

I have nothing to offer but blood, toil, tears, and sweat. You ask, 'What is our policy?' I will say, 'It is to wage war, by sea, land, and air, with all our might and with all the strength that God can give us.' ... You ask, 'What is our aim?' I can answer in one word: 'Victory'.

From a speech made by Winston Churchill in the House of Commons on 13 May 1940, three days after he became Prime Minister.

Exercise 14.5

Collect your own sources. Have you got grandparents or elderly friends who remember the war? If so, ask them what they can tell you about war work, rationing, and 'the wireless' in war-time.

Either write down what they say, or record their voices.

You could then read out what they have told you, or play your tape, to the rest of the class.

Source 14g

We shall fight on the seas and oceans. We shall fight with growing strength and confidence in the air. We shall defend our island whatever the cost may be. We shall fight on the beaches. We shall fight on the landing grounds. We shall fight in the fields and in the streets. We shall fight in the hills. We shall never surrender.

From a speech made by Winston Churchill in the House of Commons on 4 June 1940.

'... meanwhile, in Britain, the entire population, faced by the threat of invasion, has been flung into a state of complete panic...'

15 The Blitz

A Gas masks and sirens

All Britain's leaders expected the **bombing** to start as soon as the war began. Experts said, 'The bomber will always get through.' They warned that there would be massive damage in the cities, and huge numbers of dead and injured. So the government made plans to cope with the threat. Before the war started, in fact, it gave every man, woman, and child a gas-mask.

Houses with back gardens got **Anderson shelters**. (See **Source 15b**.) Brick shelters, with thick walls and concrete roofs, appeared in back-yards and school playgrounds. And the '**black-out**' came into force at once. At night, there were no street lights, and cars could show only a tiny beam. It was an offence to let a light shine from the window of a house.

A loud wail from the **siren**, rising and falling in pitch, meant 'alert — raid expected'. A long blast on a single note was the 'all clear'. As if to warn people of what was to come, the 'alert' sounded on the first morning of the war. But it was a false alarm, and was soon followed by the 'all clear'.

Evacuation began as soon as war broke out. Boys and girls between five and eleven were packed off from the cities to the 'safe' villages and country towns. Mothers with children under five were supposed to go as well. Some of the evacuees settled in well in their new homes. But for a lot of them, the countryside was strange and dull. And when no bombs fell in the first winter of the war, most of them went back home.

Now try Exercise 15.1.

Neighbours wearing gasmasks chatting over the garden fence. Neither side actually used poison gas in the Second World War.

Exercise 15.1

Read **Section A** and **Source 15c**, and look at **Sources 15a** and **15b**. Copy the sentences, and fill in the blank spaces.

a Only houses with _____ could have Anderson shelters.

b The roof of an Anderson shelter was a curved piece of _____ iron.

c The builder covered the sides and top of the iron with _____

d An Anderson shelter was big enough for _____ people.

e Children often used Anderson shelters as _____ meeting places.

f The damage in **Source 15a** was made by a _____ .

g The bomb in **Source 15a** fell only _____ _____ (two words) from the door of the Anderson shelter.

h No-one in **Source 15a** was _____ in the air-raid.

Source 15a

This family survived because they were in their Anderson shelter when a bomb exploded only ten yards away.

Source 15b

Mrs Prendergast from Clapham actually used the roof of her Anderson shelter to grow vegetables!

Source 15c

One kind of air-raid shelter was built in the garden – it was called an Anderson shelter. A builder dug a deep hole and shored up the walls with boards. Then he'd put a piece of corrugated iron over the top and fill it in with earth. It was comfortable for four, just enough for a family. Being in the shelter was like having a little den. You'd go down there, and have secret meetings, and take sweets and chocolates. It was good fun.

Adapted from words spoken by John Baker, who was seven years old at the beginning of the war.

B The London Blitz

The first big raid on London began at 5 p.m. on **7 September 1940**. It went on until 4.30 the next morning. Wave after wave of planes dropped explosives and **incendiaries** (fire bombs) on the East End. The whole of dockland was ablaze. More than 400 people were killed, and thousands were made homeless. The next night, and the next, the bombers came back. They bombed London from 7 September to 13 November — 67 nights out of 68.

Exploding bombs turned houses into **craters**. Falling **rubble** buried families and blocked the roads. The blast shattered windows in the streets around. Jagged pieces of glass flew through the air, and could cut a man or woman to shreds. Incendiaries weighed only one kilogram, but they were deadly. They started fires where they fell on the roofs of houses, shops, and warehouses. Before long, a whole district could be in flames.

As the bombs whistled down, Londoners were shocked and afraid, of course. Some, but not all, sent their children away again. Most adults stayed, and kept working. When the siren blew, they took refuge in their shelters or in the basements of big buildings. Thousands spent each night of the Blitz on the hard, crowded platforms of the **'Tube' stations**. They came out at dawn, tired, grimy, and wondering whether they still had homes.

In November 1940, the Germans turned to the cities outside London as well. On the night of 14 November, a ten-hour raid wiped out the centre of **Coventry**. Two weeks later, the middle of **Southampton** was flattened. Later, Plymouth and Liverpool got the same treatment. Almost every big city had its turn. But London was still the main target, and the raid of 10 May 1941 was the worst of the war.

Now try Exercises 15.2 and 15.3.

A London street burning in 1940, after a raid with incendiaries

Rescue workers carrying a man from the ruins of his home, where he had been trapped for 14 hours

The Blitz

Winston Churchill inspecting bomb damage in London in 1940

Exercise 15.2

Read **Section B**. Then answer the questions. Find the answers in the list below. (Some of the answers in the list are wrong.)

West End   Edinburgh   rubble   7 September 1940

three weeks   crater   explosions   fires

14 November 1940   East End   two months

Southampton

a When did the first big air-raid on London take place?
b Which was the first part of London to be bombed?
c London was bombed almost every night for how long?
d Which word means a hole caused by an exploding bomb?
e What did incendiary bombs cause?
f When did the worst raid on Coventry take place?
g Which city was badly bombed at the end of November 1940?

Source 15d

Queues formed outside the tube stations early in the morning. 'We lived only for four o'clock when they let us go down', said one man. Up to 7.30 in the evening, they had to stay at least eight feet from the platform edge. When the tubes stopped running, the light was dimmed and the current was cut off in the rail. The platforms were packed tight. People slung hammocks over the rails. Some slept on the escalators, or the bannisters between them. The snoring rose and fell like a loud wind.

Adapted from a book written by Angus Calder, who was born in 1942.

Source 15e

Sleeping in a tube station during the Blitz

Source **15f**

At night, people queued at the underground stations which were open to the public. One of them was beneath the office where I worked. To reach our private government shelter, I had to go through the public area. The smell of bodies was appalling. I held my breath, and dashed through to our air-conditioned shelter, showing my pass as I went. This was home for those civil servants, who, like me, had been bombed out of our hostels.

Written by Norah Mockler, who worked in London during the Blitz in 1940.

Exercise 15.3

Read **Sources 15d** and **15f**, and look at **Source 15e**.

a How can you be sure that **Source 15d** is not a primary source?

b Write down four facts from **Source 15d**.

c What might be the opinions of the people who sheltered in the stations about
  i the Blitz, and
  ii the tube stations?

d Write down a sentence which proves that **Source 15f** is a primary source.

e What was the author of **Source 15f**'s opinion of the tube stations?

f Write down two facts that you can learn from **Source 15e**.

A 'Doodlebug' (VI flying bomb) about to land on London in 1944. The insert shows a VI which failed to explode.

C 'Doodlebugs' and rockets

When Hitler attacked Russia in June 1941, he scaled down his air-raids on Britain. After that, the bombers came less often, and in smaller numbers. Early in 1944, the big raids did begin again, but this **'little Blitz'** lasted for only two months.

In June 1944, the first **'flying bombs'**, or **V1s**, hit London. These jet planes flew very fast, carried a big load of explosives, *and had no pilots.* A constant stream was soon flying in, by day and night. Cockneys, who called them **'Doodlebugs'**, learned to dread the moment when the engine cut out. A few seconds later, the V1 fell to earth and exploded.

Guns on the ground and fast fighters shot down some of the V1s. But there was no answer to the **rockets** which began to fall in September 1944 (**V2s**). They gave no warning at all — they just exploded. Londoners sent their children away for a third time, then tried to get on with their lives. By the end of 1944 the danger had grown less — the advancing allied armies (see Chapter 18) captured the V1 and V2 bases in France and Belgium.

Air raids killed 60,000 people in Britain. Nearly four million houses were damaged or destroyed. Hundreds of factories making planes and tanks were hit. But most of the factories were back at work in a few days. And the bombs did not break the will of the people. The Blitz left them dazed and weary, but there were no mobs in the streets demanding an end to the war.

Now try Exercises 15.4 and 15.5.

The damage caused by a V2 rocket in March 1945

Exercise 15.4

Read **Section C** and look back at **Sections A** and **B**. Write notes of your own saying what you think the results of the Blitz were. Use these headings as a guide:

a People killed.
b Houses destroyed.
c Factories damaged or destroyed.
d Children.
e People's daily lives.
f People's will to continue the war.

Exercise 15.5

Collect your own sources. Can your grandparents or elderly friends tell you anything about the Blitz? Ask them if they can remember the siren, the shelters, V1s and V2s, or can tell you stories about bomb damage. Perhaps they were children during the war, and were evacuated — ask them about that. Make notes or a tape, as you did for Exercise 14.5.

6 Occupied Europe

A The New Order

The Nazis said that the Germans were the 'master-race'. And after the conquests of 1939 to 1941, the Germans *were* the masters of Europe. The German empire swallowed a large slice of Poland and part of France. (Look at the map on page 53.) The Germans took what they wanted from the conquered lands — **coal** from the mines, **food** from the farms, and **gold** from the banks. Train-loads of great **works of art** from French galleries rolled eastward to Berlin.

Poland ceased to exist. Other states in eastern Europe learned from Poland's fate and became Germany's allies. Defeated nations in the west, such as Norway and the Netherlands, were allowed to rule themselves, as long as they obeyed the Germans. France was split in two — one half was ruled by the Germans, and the rest by a pro-German French government in **Vichy**.

As the war went on, Germany became short of **labour**. Most German men were serving in the army. So men, women, and some children from occupied countries were forced to work in German factories and mines, and on the land. The **S.S.** rounded them up and sent them off in cattle trucks. In Germany, they lived in bare barracks, and got no wages and not much to eat. A lot of them were worked to death. They were **slaves** in all but name.

The Nazis said that the **Slavs** (Russians, Poles, Czechs, etc.) were 'sub-humans'. They had no right to live except as servants of the Germans. Slavs who were not sent to Germany as slaves were to grow food for the Germans. If there was not enough food left to feed the Slavs, then they would have to starve.

Now try Exercise 16.1.

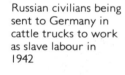
Russian civilians being sent to Germany in cattle trucks to work as slave labour in 1942

Source 16a

The Slavs are to work for us. Those we don't need may be left to die, so health services are a waste of time. Education is dangerous — every educated Slav is a future enemy. It is enough if they can count up to 100. As for food, they won't get more than they need to survive. We are the masters, so we come first.

Adapted from a letter written by Martin Bormann, Hitler's right-hand man, in July 1942.

Source 16b

I was the first doctor these women had seen for a fortnight. There were no medical supplies, even though many of them had open wounds. They had no shoes, and their only clothing was a sack, with holes for arms and head. Their hair was cut short. The food was poor, and there was very little of it. You could not enter the barracks without being attacked by fleas.

Evidence given by a German doctor who visited a slave workers' camp.

Exercise 16.1

Read **Section A** and **Sources 16a** and **16b**. Write notes answering these questions:

a Are there any facts in **Source 16a**?
b What was Martin Bormann's opinion of the Germans?
c What, in Bormann's opinion, was the duty of the Slavs?
d What did Bormann think about
   i health care for the Slavs,
   ii education for the Slavs,
   iii food supplies for the Slavs?
e How many facts can you find in **Source 16b**?
f Does **Source 16b** contain any opinions? What do you think the doctor's opinions were?

All Jews under Nazi control were forced to wear a yellow Star of David, so that they could be identified

B The Holocaust

The Nazis hated **Jews**. By 1939, Jews had lost all normal rights in Germany. As the German army spread Hitler's rule, anti-Jewish laws were enforced in more and more countries. After the conquest of Poland, all Polish Jews were forced to live in a walled-off part of Warsaw, called the '**ghetto**'. Before long, all the Jews in Hitler's Europe were sent to **concentration camps**.

At first, the Nazis used the Jews in the camps as slave labour. But in 1940 or 1941, Hitler decided on 'the final solution of the Jewish question'. These few words were a sentence of death for a whole race. To carry it out, **Auschwitz**, **Chelmno**, **Treblinka**, etc. (all in what had been Poland) became '**killing camps**'.

Jews are rounded up by German soldiers in the Warsaw ghetto

This is what British troops found when they liberated Belsen concentration camp in 1945

Jewish men, women, and children arrived at the camps in tightly-packed railway trucks. Guards picked out some for **forced labour**, but sent most straight to the 'showers'. Groups of frightened Jews had to strip naked, and walk into bare sheds which were not showers, but **gas chambers**. The doors were slammed and locked behind them. Then poison-gas began to seep from the ceiling. When they were all dead, special troops cleared out the bodies, and removed the gold fillings from their teeth. (Read **Source 16c**.)

The mass-murder of the Jews is called the '**Holocaust**'. Not all the victims died in the camps. Special S.S. units followed the Germany army into Russia, to find and shoot the Russian Jews. But the gas chambers were the main killers. Well over two million people died in Auschwitz alone. And the final death-toll of the Holocaust was **between four and six million** Jews.

Now try Exercise 16.2.

Source 16c

We dropped a prussic acid crystal into the death chamber from a small hole. It took from three to fifteen minutes to kill all the people in the chamber. We knew when they were dead because their screaming stopped. After about half an hour, we opened the doors and took the bodies out. Then special squads took the rings off the corpses and pulled out their gold teeth.

Evidence given by Rudolf Hoess, a former commander at Auschwitz, at his trial in 1946.

Exercise 16.2

Read **Section B** and **Source 16c**.
Complete the sentences in your own
words.

a When the Germans had conquered
   Poland, the Polish Jews ...
b Later, all Jews in the countries the
   Germans had conquered ...
c 'The final solution of the Jewish
   question' meant ...
d Auschwitz, Chelmno and Treblinka
   were ...
e The Nazi guards at Auschwitz
   pretended that ...
f In 1946, Rudolf Hoess admitted ...
g The word 'Holocaust' means ...
h The total number of Holocaust
   victims was ...

C Resistance

Not everyone in the conquered countries thought that the war was lost. Some escaped to England, to continue the fight. Others stayed at home and joined the **resistance**. As time passed, and it became clear that in the end the allies would win, the resistance groups grew bigger and stronger.

Some resisters fought the Germans. In the mountains of Yugoslavia, the **partisans** led by **Marshal Tito** waged a full-scale war. With the help of arms dropped by the allies, they took control of whole towns and districts. Thousands of German troops, with tanks and heavy guns, could not beat them. The partisans played a big part in driving the Germans from their country.

The French and Belgian resistance groups ran **'escape lines'** for allied airmen who had been shot down. They dressed them as Frenchmen, gave them forged papers, and passed them on to the next group. With the help of these brave men and women, hundreds of airmen escaped to neutral Spain. From there they got back to Britain. Resistance workers who were caught by the Gestapo were tortured, then shot.

Resistance groups in France kept in touch with London by **radio**. They passed back news about numbers of German troops, planes, etc. London sent out arms, explosives, and agents to help and lead them. In the same way, Russian partisans behind the German lines got orders from Moscow. Then, risking certain death if they were caught, they blew up bridges, trains, and arms dumps to hold up the German advance.

Now try Exercises 16.3 and 16.4.

Source 16d

French resistance
fighters learn how to
use weapons dropped
to them by parachute
by the allies

Exercise 16.3

Read **Section C**, then answer the questions in sentences.

a What do you think were the motives of people who joined the resistance?

b Why did the allies send arms to Tito's partisans?

c Why did allied airmen who had been shot down want to reach Spain?

d Why did the Gestapo torture captured resistance workers?

e Why did French resistance groups keep in touch with London by radio?

f Why did the Russian generals think that the partisans were important?

Draw two or three cartoon pictures, with pin-men if you wish, showing some of the things resistance groups did.

Source **16e**

Criminals in the pay of England and Russia killed the German commander of Nantes on 20 October. Up to now the killers have not been caught. To pay for this crime, I have ordered that 50 hostages should be shot. If the killers are not handed over by 23 October, 50 more will be shot.

German army notice in a French newspaper on 22 October 1941.

Exercise 16.4

Read **Source 16e** and look at **Sources 16d** and **16f**. Write three paragraphs:

a Are **Sources 16d**, **16e** and **16f** primary or secondary sources? Give reasons for your answer.

b What had happened in Nantes (**Source 16e**)? Who do you think the 'criminals' were? Why did the Germans blame England and Russia? Why were the hostages shot? What would be the effect on the French people?

c Describe what you can see in **Sources 16d** and **16f**. Give at least two details from each source.

Source **16f**

Russian partisans prepare to blow up a railway line behind German lines

17 Inside Germany

A Work and food

As the war went on, the German army needed more and more men, to take the places of the killed and wounded. In 1944, the government said that all boys and men from sixteen to sixty had to join the army or the home defence force. Only the most skilled workers were exempt.

But the factories had to have workers to keep the machines running. The places left empty by the men who had gone to war were partly filled by **foreign workers**. (See Chapter 16.) But still there were gaps, so in 1943 **girls** and **women** between seventeen and forty-five were called up. And in the next year, the age limit was raised to fifty. (The mothers of young children could stay at home.)

The government also controlled the supplies of **food**. It rationed bread, but said that miners and other 'heavy' workers could have twice the normal share. And as in Britain, bread was made from less pure flour than before the war. A further move was to tell shops not to sell bread until it was one day old — older bread needs more chewing!

Meat, eggs, butter, and sugar were all rationed in Germany, as they were in Britain. And the amount allowed got less as the end of the war came closer. By 1944, German adults got no sugar at all. Most of the 'coffee' in the shops was artificial — made from acorns, it was said.

A recruitment poster for the German Home Guard

Germans who had enough money could get sugar and real coffee. But they had to go to the **'black market'** traders, who broke all the rationing rules. 'Black market' prices were sky-high, of course. In 1945, with Germany in ruins, goods were exchanged for cigarettes, not money. Farmers sold eggs directly to the public, at one cigarette per egg.

Now try Exercise 17.1.

Exercise 17.1

Read **Section A**. Write sentences to show that you know what these words and phrases mean:

called up   age limit   rationed   'heavy' workers

artificial   black market   sky-high

B Air-raids

The allied bombing of Germany was like the German 'Blitz' on Britain, but much worse. The Blitz grew less severe after 1941, but the allied raids got bigger. The first **thousand-bomber raid** was on Cologne in May 1942. And in 1944, the allies dropped ten times as many bombs as in 1942.

The bombing was worst in **Berlin**, **Hamburg** and the **Ruhr** coal-field. Women and children from those places were sent to the country districts for safety. Townsfolk and the country people did not get on, though, so a drift back to the towns began. But those who returned sometimes could not find their homes. Their old streets were no more than heaps of rubble.

With the help of Dr. Goebbels and his propaganda (see Chapter 7), the Germans kept their spirits up. Goebbels, through the press and radio, told the Germans that they must not give in. If they lost the war, the allies would treat them as slaves. And although the bombing was bad, Hitler had **secret weapons** which would soon turn the tide.

In some places, such as **Dresden**, the Germans' spirits did crack in the last weeks of the war. Early in 1945, Dresden was full of refugees, fleeing as the Russians advanced. On 13 and 14 February, allied bombers destroyed the heart of the city. Mass incendiaries caused a '**fire-storm**' which burned thousands to death. More than 100,000 people died in the raid.

Now try Exercises 17.2 and 17.3.

Source 17a

Dresden after an air raid in 1945

90

Source 17b

The siren went shortly before 1 a.m. Before we could reach the shelter, a thunderstorm of noise exploded above us. It didn't stop even for a second, one bang after another. The house shook and the windows trembled. For two whole hours, this ear-splitting terror went on. No-one spoke. We all waited for the worst with each massive explosion. Heads went down each time there was a crash, and faces were trapped in horror.

A description of an allied air-raid on Hamburg in 1943, adapted from the diary of Mathilde Wolff-Mönckeberg.

Source 17c

You felt fright, sheer fright, the first time you saw a great barrage of flak in front of you. All the searchlights were weaving, then holding together like a pyramid of light. You were like a moth caught in the centre of it. But the business of fighting and flying your aircraft is the best antidote to fear that there is.

Adapted from the words of an R.A.F. pilot, 'Micky' Martin.

Dresden in 1949 – four years after the end of the war. The physical effects of the bombing lasted a long time.

Exercise 17.2

Read **Section B** and **Sources 17b** and **17c**. Discuss the questions in a group:

a The two sources describe an air-raid from which two points of view?

b What were the worst things about the air-raid in **Source 17b**?

c How do you know that there was a light in the shelter?

d For the author of **Source 17c**, what were the **worst** things about a raid?

e How did the author of **Source 17c** overcome his fear?

Either make notes so that you can tell the rest of the class what you think, or make a tape.

91

Source **17d**

A German anti-Jewish poster. The Jew is hiding behind the flags of Britain, the U.S.A. and Communist Russia. The words mean 'Behind the enemy powers: the Jew'.

Exercise 17.3

Look at **Sources 17a** and **17d**. Answer the questions.

a Which source is a photograph, and which is a propaganda poster?
b When and where was the photograph taken?
c Which facts can we learn from the photograph? (Find at least two.)
d Which flags can you see in **Source 17d**?
e What do the flags stand for?
f How can you recognize the Jew in **Source 17d**?
g What was **Source 17d** trying to make the Germans believe?

C Germans against Hitler

As a rule, Germans who did not like Hitler kept quiet. (If they said what they thought, they were soon arrested.) In fact, thanks to Dr. Goebbels, most Germans followed Hitler gladly. But there were students, ex-trade union men, and church leaders who were against the Nazis. And as the war started to go badly, some **army officers** began to think of a change.

The officers who planned to get rid of Hitler wanted to end the war with **Britain** and the **U.S.A.** But they meant to continue the war with **Russia**. And they hoped that Germany would be able to keep most of the extra land that Hitler had won. (This plan could never have worked. Churchill and Roosevelt would not have let down their ally Stalin. And the allies were bound to take back the land that Hitler had seized.)

There were at least six plots to kill Hitler in 1943. But the most famous attempt on the Führer's life took place in July 1944 at Hitler's **'Wolf's Lair'** headquarters. An army colonel left a case containing a bomb under a table in a room where Hitler was due to meet his staff. The bomb went off and injured Hitler, but it did not kill him.

Most of Germany's top generals knew about the plan. But when the bomb failed to kill Hitler, the plot collapsed. The Gestapo and S.S. moved in and rounded up the 'traitors'. A total of 5,000, most of them officers, were put to death. (Even Rommel, the 'Desert Fox', was in the plot. He was allowed to take his own life.) Hitler never trusted the army again.

Now try Exercises 17.4 and 17.5.

Exercise 17.4

Read **Section C**. Write out the sentences, filling in the blank spaces.

a Germans who spoke out against Hitler were usually _____

b Some students, former _____ _____ leaders and priests disliked Hitler.

c Some army officers wanted to end the war against _____ and the _____

d These officers hoped that Germany would be able to keep most of the _____ that Hitler had won.

e The officers decided that they must try to _____ Hitler.

f A bomb plot at the _____ _____ headquarters in July 1944 nearly killed Hitler.

g After the bomb plot, the Gestapo arrested _____ 'traitors'.

Source 17e

At 12.42 the bomb exploded with a great crash. Most of the roof of the building fell in, and all the windows were blown out. There was chaos inside. The secretary, Berger, was killed. Three officers died from their injuries. Two others were badly wounded. Hitler had his hair set on fire, his right leg badly burned, his right arm paralysed for a while, and both ear drums damaged. But he was alive.

Adapted from a book written by Terence Prittie in 1964.

Source 17f

Hitler got out of the smoking wreckage with a blackened face and the back of his head singed. His trousers hung in shreds, and he was covered in dust. His right elbow was bleeding, and he had a few slight bruises on his left hand. Both his ear drums were damaged, but he lost his hearing only for a short time. His legs were the worst — splinters of wood had been driven into the flesh. But the trembling in his left leg soon stopped. Of the 24 persons in the room, only four were badly injured.

Adapted from a book written by Joachim Fest in 1973.

Exercise 17.5

Read **Sources 17e** and **17f**. Compare these two accounts of the attempt on Hitler's life on 20 July 1944. Do they say the same things? Are the details different? Write paragraphs in your own words about:

a Hitler's appearance and injuries.
b What happened to the other people in the building.

Hitler is showing Mussolini the damage to his headquarters after the failure of the July bomb plot

18 Victory in Europe

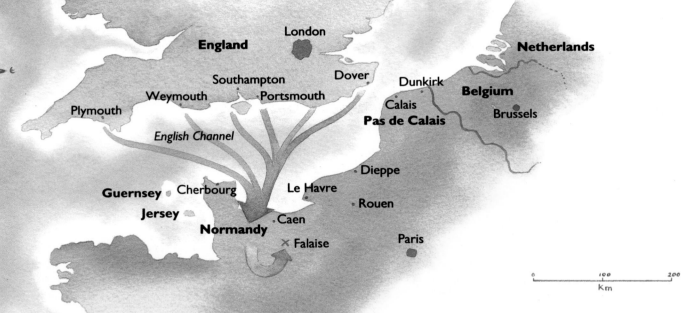

A The Normandy invasion

Occupied by Germans up to June 1944

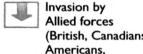
Invasion by Allied forces (British, Canadians, Americans, Free French, etc.)

Churchill and Roosevelt agreed that they had to deal with Germany first, then with Japan. To beat the Germans, they had to invade France. So all through 1942 and 1943, American troops and arms were sent to Britain. Late in 1943, the two leaders decided to invade France in the spring of 1944. They put an American, **General Eisenhower** ('Ike' to his men) in charge. The operation's code-name was '**Overlord**'.

'Ike' knew that the Germans would expect the allies to land in the Pas de Calais. (Look at the map.) So to deceive them, he chose **Normandy** as the target for 'Overlord'. For the job, he had three million men, 3,000 ships, and 13,000 planes. Two floating concrete harbours ('**Mulberries**') were to be towed across to France. A pipe-line ('**Pluto**') was to carry oil under the sea. It was going to be the biggest invasion in history.

Bad weather held up the plans at first. Then, on the night of **5–6 June 1944**, allied paratroops dropped behind the German lines. At dawn, the first landing-craft reached the beaches. Thousands of men, tanks, and guns poured ashore. Aircraft bombed the Germans, while big guns on the warships pounded them with shells. The Germans had to give ground, and 'Ike's army got a foothold in France.

After two months of hard fighting, the allies won a great victory at **Falaise**. The Germans collapsed. A huge retreat began, and the allied tanks rushed forward. On 24 August, '**Free French**' troops entered Paris. The French people went wild with delight. On 3 September, British and Canadian troops were mobbed by happy Belgians in Brussels.

Now try Exercises 18.1 and 18.2.

Source 18a

The allied ships are close packed and stretching as far as the eye can see. I see flashes as their guns open up. The sea between the beach and the ships is dark blue. There are white lines on the water, coming from the ships. These are the landing craft, which spew up brown groups of soldiers as they touch down on the beach. I see white fountains of water rise — our coastal guns. We see brown figures, struggling through the sand dunes. They are wearing flat helmets — British soldiers. Then I notice tanks, one, two, three, a whole group of them.

Adapted from the report of a German officer in Normandy on 6 June 1944.

Exercise 18.1

Read **Section A**, look at the map, and look at **Source 18b**. Write down the answers to the questions.

a Which general was in charge of the invasion of France? What was the invasion plan's code-name?

b Why did the allies invade Normandy, and not the Pas de Calais?

c What were 'Mulberries'?

d What was 'Pluto'?

e When was 'D-Day'?

f How many ships were there in the 'D-Day' fleet?

g What can you see above the ships in **Source 18b**? What were they for?

h What else can you see in **Source 18b**? (Write down as many things as possible.)

i What happened at Falaise?

j Why were the people of Paris and Brussels so pleased?

Draw a sketch-map of southern England and northern France. Mark the main towns, Normandy, the Pas de Calais, and the route of the allied invasion.

Source 18b

One of the 'D-Day' invasion beaches. D-Day was 6 June 1944, the start of the Normandy invasion

Source 18c

As we approached the beach, the whistle of bullets could be heard above the crash of the waves. . . . Some of the troops stumbled into the surf. Others were more lucky and landed dry, holding their rifles above their heads. . . . The dash by the men from the boats to the beach took a heavy toll. But to delay meant certain death. Those who realized this kept moving inland.

Adapted from a British officer's account.

Exercise 18.2

Read **Source 18a** (which will be called 'the German source') and **Sources 18c** and **18d** (which will be called 'the British sources'). Write notes to answer the questions.

a Which facts can you find in the German source and in one of the British sources?
b Which facts can you find only in the German source?
c Which facts can you find only in the British sources?

Source 18d

As the day slowly dawned, we saw that the shadow behind us was a solid mass of ships. They began to bombard the coast, and their shellbursts threw up great mushrooms of dust and debris. Overhead, a stream of heavy bombers flew in to blast the defences. A huge pall of smoke spread over the coast. The noise was appalling. . . . From time to time gigantic columns of water shot up and proved that the enemy guns were still in action.

Adapted from a British naval officer's account of the Normandy invasion.

B The Russian advance

The war in Russia was on a huge scale. The front stretched more than 2,000 miles from north to south. In 1943, the Germans had five million men there (two-thirds of their army). On the other side, the Russian army was even bigger, and growing all the time. And the Russian factories were turning out tanks, guns, and aircraft at a rate the Germans could not match.

After Stalingrad (see Chapter 10), the Russians knew that they could beat the Germans. In July 1943, they won the biggest tank battle of the war at **Kursk**. In late 1943 and the first months of 1944, they drove the Germans out of southern Russia. Then in June 1944, at the same time as 'Overlord', they advanced into Poland.

On 1 August 1944, the Russians reached the edge of **Warsaw**, the Polish capital. On that same day, the Poles in Warsaw rose in revolt against the Germans. Britain and the U.S.A. sent some help by air to the Poles, but the Russians made no move until it was too late. The revolt lasted two months. In that time, about 50,000 Poles were killed or wounded, and 90 per cent of Warsaw was destroyed.

The Russians swept through the Balkans. They made Hitler's allies, **Romania** and **Bulgaria**, drop out of the war. Then, with the help of Tito's partisans, they forced the Germans to flee from **Yugoslavia**. By the end of 1944, they had reached Hungary. (Look at the map.)

Now try Exercise 18.3.

Right: Members of the Polish Home Army moving through the Warsaw ghetto during the Warsaw rising in 1944. The flag above them is the Polish flag.

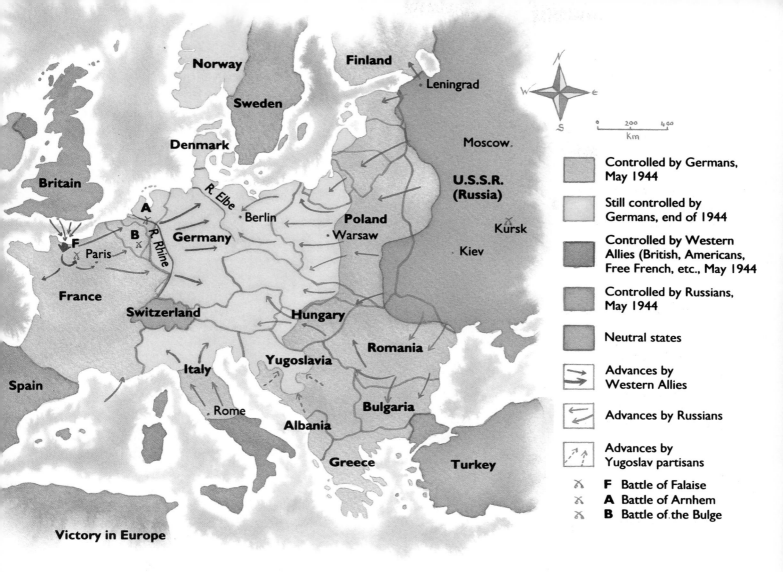

Norway

Finland

Sweden

Leningrad

Denmark

Britain

Moscow

U.S.S.R.
(Russia)

R. Elbe

A

Berlin

Poland

Kursk

F

B R. Rhine

Germany

Warsaw

Paris

Kiev

France

Switzerland

Hungary

Romania

Spain

Italy

Yugoslavia

Rome

Bulgaria

Albania

Greece

Turkey

Victory in Europe

Controlled by Germans, May 1944

Still controlled by Germans, end of 1944

Controlled by Western Allies (British, Americans, Free French, etc., May 1944

Controlled by Russians, May 1944

Neutral states

Advances by Western Allies

Advances by Russians

Advances by Yugoslav partisans

F Battle of Falaise

A Battle of Arnhem

B Battle of the Bulge

Russian tanks advancing in the Ukraine, 1943

Source 18e

Russian soldiers are welcomed by liberated Polish villagers in 1944

Source 18g

Russian and American troops link up on the River Elbe in Germany in April 1945

Source 18f

We were taken from our truck ... A (Russian) officer came along and selected those who were to die ... We others were ordered back to our wagons and told to watch. An execution squad of ten soldiers shot the victims as they knelt in the snow, begging for their lives.

The words of a German refugee, fleeing from the Russian army in 1945. Many others told the same kind of story. Some were a great deal worse.

Exercise 18.3

Read **Section B** and **Source 18f**, and look at **Sources 18e** and **18g**.

a What do we learn about Russian soldiers from
   i **Source 18f**,
   ii **Sources 18e** and **18g**.
b Should we believe what the photographs tell us? (Write a sentence.)
c Should we believe the written source (**Source 18f**)? (Write at least one sentence, giving your reasons.)
d Can we believe all three of these sources? (Write two or three sentences, giving your reasons.)

C The German surrender

In August 1944, the British, Canadians, and Americans were advancing from the west. The Russians were not far from the German border in the east. It looked as though the end was near for Hitler and his 'Reich'. But the German army was not finished yet. Between 17 and 30 September, it won a victory at **Arnhem** in Holland, where it stopped the British from taking and holding a key bridge over the River Rhine.

And in December 1944, the Germans made one last attempt to win the war. They attacked the Americans at the weakest point in their line, in the Ardennes forest in Belgium. This was the '**Battle of the Bulge**'. The Germans advanced a few miles, but their tanks came to a stop when they ran out of fuel. Within a month, the allies had won back the lost ground.

In March 1945, the western allies crossed the **Rhine**. There was now no hope for Hitler. The allied armies poured eastwards, north and south of the Ruhr, cutting the German army off from the factories which supplied it. At the same time, the Russians advanced from Poland into Germany. On 21 April, they reached the outskirts of **Berlin**. Four days later, Russian and U.S. troops met on the River Elbe.

Hitler was now a sick and broken man. He blamed the German people for his defeat — he said they had failed their leader. On 30 April, with the Russians only two blocks from his headquarters, he took his life. On his orders, his body was burned and the ashes scattered. A week later, the German armed forces surrendered, and the war was over.

Now try Exercise 18.4.

Exercise 18.4

Read **Section C**. Then find events to go with these dates. (You will need to look at **Sections A** and **B** as well as **Section C**.) Write out the events and dates.

a 6 June 1944
b 1 August 1944
c 24 August 1944
d 3 September 1944
e 17–30 September 1944
f December 1944
g March 1945
h 21 April 1945
i 30 April 1945
j 7 May 1945

The happy inmates of Dachau concentration camp on the day the American army arrived

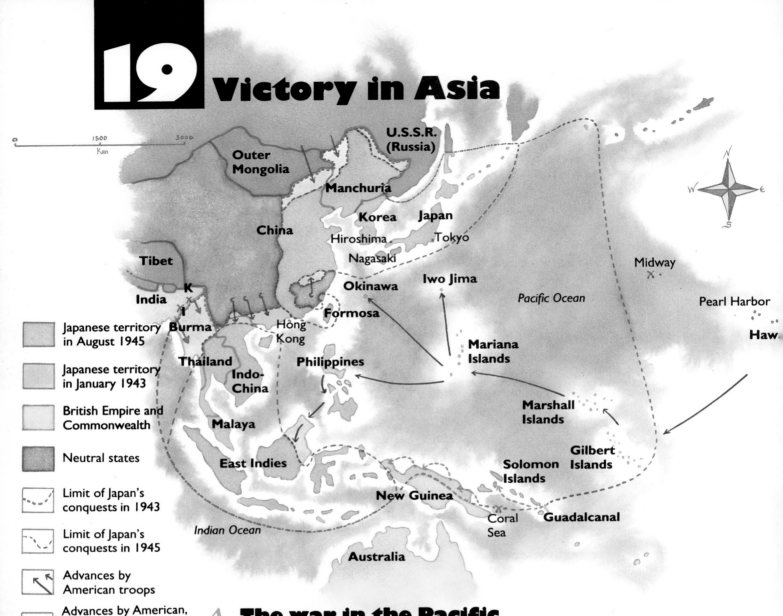

Map legend:
- Japanese territory in August 1945
- Japanese territory in January 1943
- British Empire and Commonwealth
- Neutral states
- Limit of Japan's conquests in 1943
- Limit of Japan's conquests in 1945
- Advances by American troops
- Advances by American, Australian, & New Zealand troops
- Advances by Chinese troops
- Advances by British and Commonwealth troops
- Advances by Russian troops, August 1945
- K X Battle of Kohima
- I X Battle of Imphal

Note:
Russia declared war on Japan on 8 August 1945, six days before Japan surrendered

A The war in the Pacific

For six months after Pearl Harbor, Japan had nothing but success. (See Chapter 11.) Then in May 1942, in the battle of the **Coral Sea**, the U.S. fleet brought the string of victories to an end. The battle was a draw, but it stopped the Japanese advance. (Look at the map.)

The battle of the Coral Sea (and the battle of **Midway**, a month later) showed that a change had taken place in war at sea. The great battleships with their mighty guns, were no longer a fleet's main strength. What mattered now were the **aircraft carriers**, and

their planes. At Midway, the Americans sank all four of Japan's carriers. They won the battle, broke Japan's grip on the Pacific, and made sure that Japan would lose the war.

From late 1942, men from the U.S.A., Australia, and New Zealand slowly took back the land that Japan had seized. The battles were always fierce — the Japanese preferred death to surrender. During 1943, the armies pushed forward through the jungles of **New Guinea**. And the U.S. marines advanced from island to island, at great cost to human life.

In October 1944, U.S. troops landed in the Philippines. It took four more months to conquer these islands, though. Then came **Iwo Jima**, where 23,000 Japanese fought to the last man, and 20,000 Americans died, all for eight square miles. And in mid-1945, 'Kamikaze' pilots appeared. These heroes (or madmen) dived their planes, full of bombs, straight onto allied ships.

Japan's soldiers, sailors, and airmen were very brave, but the war was lost. At home in Japan, life got grimmer day by day. The cities were now within the range of allied bombers. And allied submarines had sunk most of the merchant ships that brought in food and oil.

Now try Exercises 19.1 and 19.2.

Source **19b**

American aircraft dropping bombs on Japan

Exercise 19.1

Read **Section A** and look at the map. Then write out the sentences below, and add either TRUE or FALSE after each of them.

a The battle of the Coral Sea was fought in the Indian Ocean.
b Aircraft carriers were the most important ships in the battle of Midway.
c The battle of Midway was fought in June 1942.
d New Guinea lies to the west of Australia.
e American troops won back control of the Philippines in late 1944 and early 1945.
f More than 40,000 men died in the battle for Iwo Jima.
g Japanese submarines sank most of the allies' merchant ships.

Draw a picture of an American bomber.

Exercise 19.2

Look at **Sources 19a**, **19b** and **19c**. Then write a paragraph about each of the sources. In each case, say what is happening (include two or more details from each photograph). Also, say whether you think that the photographs were taken as the fighting was going on, and give your reasons.

B Burma and China

Hong Kong, Malaya, Burma, and India were all British when war with Japan broke out in 1941. The Japanese quickly seized Hong Kong and Malaya. By April 1942, they had conquered **Burma** as well. Their army stood on the borders of India. Their fleet sailed freely in the Indian Ocean. Planes from their carriers bombed Britain's bases in Ceylon (now Sri Lanka).

For the next two years, the Japanese army did not move forward. The British Fourteenth Army defending a range of hills clad in thick **jungle** stood between them and India. The jungle was an unhealthy and hostile place. As well as the normal dangers of war, it held mosquitoes that spread disease, blood-sucking leeches, and poisonous snakes. The British soldiers' spirits were low. They called themselves 'the forgotten army'.

In March 1944, the Japanese at last did try to advance. This time, they did not win a quick victory. The British stood firm in the battles of **Imphal** and **Kohima**, which lasted four months. When the monsoon rains stopped in October, they began to advance. The Japanese retreat became a collapse. By June 1945, almost all of Burma was back in British hands.

Source 19c

A Japanese 'Kamikaze' plane is shot down just before reaching its target

In the last months of the war, the British in Burma got some help from China. By 1945, the Chinese had been at war with Japan for eight years. (See Chapter 11.) Now they were worn out, and not able to fight much more. But Japan needed troops to control the large parts of China it had seized. So these men were not free to fight China's western allies.

Now try Exercise 19.3.

Exercise 19.3

Read **Section B**. Write sentences to show that you know what these words and phrases mean. (Use a dictionary if necessary.)

at will   carriers   jungle   mosquitoes   leeches
low spirits   stood firm   monsoon

British troops advancing through the jungle in Burma

C The atomic bomb

In mid-1944, **Tojo** resigned as Prime Minister of Japan. The new leaders heard nothing but reports of defeats. And they could not fail to see the fires caused by the air-raids on their cities. (Most Japanese houses were made of wood.) In May 1945, the war in Europe ended. The U.S.A. and Britain would soon turn their full strength on Japan. And Russia might well join them in the Far East war.

To the allies, though, the war was far from won. Japan still held a large part of China and south-east Asia. Experts thought that it would take eighteen months to conquer all this land and invade Japan. They said that winning the war would cost a further million allied soldiers' lives.

All this was changed by the **atomic bomb**. By mid-1945, scientists in the U.S.A. had made three bombs. They tested one in the desert of New Mexico in July. Then on 6 August, a B-29 bomber dropped the second one on **Hiroshima**. The effect was like 20,000 tons of high explosive — the whole city was wiped out. Three days later, the third bomb destroyed **Nagasaki**. (Read **Source 19d**.)

The Japanese did not know that there were no more bombs. They were ready for peace in any case. But the allies said that they must surrender with no conditions. Japan wanted just one condition — that the **emperor** should stay on his throne. In the end, it was the emperor himself who decided. Japan surrendered with no conditions on 14 August 1945.

Now try Exercises 19.4 and 19.5.

Source **19d**

I was looking up into the sky, trying to spot the plane. Then I saw a big flash, so I hid my face on the ground. I remember that I must have been blown over by the impact. When I came round, I couldn't find any of my friends. They were either blown to bits or burned. All my clothes were torn away. My skin just peeled off and was hanging from my body.

Adapted from the words of a survivor of Hiroshima.

Hiroshima after the
atomic bomb

Source 19e

a *The allies knew that an invasion of Japan would
cost a lot of lives.*
b *Japan's leaders were ready to surrender. They
thought that if the allies invaded Japan, they
would get rid of the emperor when they had
won.*
c *The Americans knew that Japan wanted peace.*
d *If the atomic bomb had been dropped on open
country, the effect on Japan's leaders would have
been the same.*
e *The Russians went to war with Japan on 8
August 1945. This had as much effect on Japan
as the atomic bomb.*

Ideas from a book written by Richard Storry in 1960.
These are not Mr Storry's own words.

Exercise 19.4

Read **Section C** and **Sources 19e** and **19f**, then discuss
these questions in a group:

a Which ideas can you find in both sources?
b Which ideas can you find only in **Source 19e**?
c Which ideas can you find only in **Source 19f**?
d Do **you** think that the Americans were right to drop the
atomic bomb on two Japanese cities?
Either **i** Make notes, so that one person can tell the rest of
the class what your group thinks, or **ii** Make a tape,
giving your group's answer.

Source 19f

a *People in the U.S.A. believed
that it would take a long
time to invade and conquer
Japan. And they thought that
a lot of soldiers would be
killed.*
b *Japan's leaders let the allies
know that they wanted
peace. But they were not
ready to surrender without
conditions. (They wanted to
keep their emperor.)*
c *You could say that the
atomic bombs cost less loss
of life to Japan than an
invasion would have done.*
d *Russia's entry into the war
against Japan was less
important than the atomic
bomb.*
e *The U.S.A. wanted to end
the war as soon as possible.*

Ideas from a book written by A. J. P.
Taylor in 1965. These are not Mr
Taylor's own words.

20 Divided Europe

A Tehran, Yalta and Potsdam

During the war, Stalin was never on good terms with Churchill and Roosevelt. He was not grateful for the aid the western leaders sent him. He thought that they should have invaded occupied France much sooner than they did. He said that they wanted Russia to win the war for them. He was sure that Russia suffered far more in damage and lives lost than Britain or the U.S.A.

The 'big three' met at **Tehran** in Iran in late 1943, and at **Yalta** in southern Russia in early 1945. At Tehran, they discussed how they would win the war. At Yalta, they knew the war was won. So their talk was about Europe after the war. They agreed that, for a time at least, they would share the job of governing Germany among them.

The next meeting was at **Potsdam**, just outside Berlin, in July 1945, when the war in Europe was over. By then,

Roosevelt was dead, and **Harry Truman** was President of the U.S.A.. And half-way through the meeting, the results of the British election became known. Labour had won, so **Clement Attlee**, the new Prime Minister, took Churchill's place at Potsdam.

Truman and Attlee did not like what Stalin said at Potsdam. (He told them that he would keep the eastern half of **Poland**, which he had seized in 1939.) In return, he wanted to give Poland a slice of German land. (Look at the map on page 106.) And he said that the Germans must pay, with machines and goods, for the damage they had done in Russia. The leaders agreed on one thing — the Nazi leaders they had captured would **go on trial** for their crimes.

Now try Exercise 20.1.

The 'big three' at the Tehran conference: Churchill (left), Roosevelt (centre), and Stalin (right)

Russia before 1939

Land seized by Russia between 1939 and 1945

Other countries with Communist governments in 1950

Neutral countries

Countries which joined NATO in 1949

Countries which joined NATO between 1950 and 1955 (with dates)

Land taken from Germany by Poland in 1945

Russian zone of Austria, 1945-1955

0   200   400 km

Europe after the Second World War

A poster printed in Dresden in the Russian Zone of Germany in November 1945. The words say 'The end of 12 years of Hitler rule'.

Exercise 20.1

Read **Section A**. Then complete the sentences **a** to **g** by choosing from the list of 'second halves' below. Write out the complete sentences.

a Stalin thought that Russia . . .
b At Yalta, the allies agreed to share . . .
c Harry Truman became . . .
d Clement Attlee became . . .
e At Potsdam, Stalin said that Russia was going to . . .
f Stalin said that the Germans had to pay . . .
g At Potsdam, the allies agreed . . .

'Second halves'
● President of the U.S.A. when Roosevelt died.
● for the damage their armies had done in Russia.
● suffered more than its allies in the war.
● keep the eastern half of Poland.
● the task of ruling Germany after the war.
● to put the leading Nazis on trial.
● British Prime Minister after the election in 1945.

B The division of Germany

The 'big three' decided in 1945 to divide Germany into three **zones**. Russia would be in charge of the east, Britain of the north-west, and the U.S.A. of the south-west. Berlin, the capital, was in the Russian zone, but each of the allies took control of a '**sector**' there. (Later, France was given a zone in the west, and a sector in Berlin.)

The allies wiped out all traces of the Nazi party, and abolished the German armed forces. But they gave the Germans some say in their own affairs. In 1946, there were elections for town and county councils in all of the zones. In western Germany, the elections were free for all parties except the Nazis. In eastern Germany, the Russians made sure that the **Communists** won.

Ill-feeling grew between East and West. From June 1948 to May 1949, the Russians tried to make the Western powers give up their sectors of **Berlin**. They stopped the movement of all Berlin's traffic by road and rail to the western zones. In reply, British and Americans planes brought in all the food and fuel that the people of West Berlin needed. (There were more than 800 flights a day.) In the end, the Russians opened up the land routes again.

These events pushed the former allies further apart. In 1949, the U.S.A., Britain and France turned their zones into a **West German state**. The new republic was a **democracy**, with a freely elected parliament that met in Bonn. The Russians replied by making their zone into an **East German state**. (Its capital was Berlin.) In elections in the east, the **Communists** always won. This split between East and West Germany lasted for forty years.

Now try Exercise 20.2.

Exercise 20.2

Read **Section B**. Make notes, saying what were the results for Germany of

a The decisions taken by the 'big three' in 1945.
b Growing ill-feeling between Russia and the West.

The Berlin airlift, 1948. British and American aircraft brought in West Berlin's food and fuel for almost a year.

C The Cold War

President Truman had not planned to keep American troops in Europe once the war was over. But because of Stalin, he changed his mind. Stalin had seized extra land for Russia at the expense of his neighbours to the west. (Look at the map.) And Stalin now made sure that all the states of Eastern Europe were ruled by Communists. This meant that they all took orders from **Moscow**.

Most people in the West were alarmed. They said that Stalin was acting like Hitler in the 1930s. They thought Stalin's aim was to control the whole of Europe if he could. They saw his take-over in Eastern Europe as part of a grand plan to spread Communism to all corners of the world.

It may be true that Stalin was trying to **expand**. On the other hand, his aim could have been **defence**. Perhaps the ring of states with Communists in control was just a way of protecting Russia. Russia had suffered greatly from the German invasion in 1941. Stalin said that putting Russian troops in Poland, Hungary, etc. was just a way of making sure that it did not happen again.

The British were sure that Russia was a threat. By 1948, they were glad to find that the Americans agreed. (Only the U.S.A. was strong enough to stand up to the Russians.) In April 1949, the U.S.A., Britain, and six other Western states formed the North Atlantic Treaty Organisation (**NATO**). NATO's aim was to protect Western Europe from a Russian attack. And for the next forty years, there was a '**Cold War**' between East and West.

Now try Exercises 20.3 and 20.4.

Exercise 20.3

Read **Section C**, and look at **Sources 20a** and **20c**. Write out the sentences, and add either TRUE or FALSE after each of them.

a President Truman kept American troops in Europe because he did not trust Stalin.
b Truman and Stalin used to play poker once a week.
c Stalin used to cheat at cards.
d The 'Atlantic Pact' was another name for NATO.
e President Truman was the leader of the NATO allies.
f People in the West thought that Stalin was crafty and cunning.
g West Germans used to try to escape to the East.
h East German guards used to shoot people who tried to escape to the West.
i For East Germans, West Berlin was an escape route.

Source 20a

David Low's cartoon shows Stalin and Truman playing poker. The other western leaders are sitting behind Truman. ('Atlantic Pact' is another name for NATO.)

Source 20b

The Western states send spies, assassins, and wreckers into our country. They are just waiting for a chance to attack it with armed force. We must remember that we are surrounded by people and governments who hate us. At all times, we are just a hair's breadth from invasion. We must take every chance to get rid of non-Communist governments in other states.

Adapted from words written by Joseph Stalin in 1940.

Source 20d

Stalin told me that the plains of Poland were the invasion route of Europe to Russia. So he had to control Poland. It was fear. He didn't want to see a united Germany. Stalin made it clear to me – I spoke with him many times – that they could not afford to let Germany build up again. They'd been invaded twice, and he was not willing to let it happen again.

Adapted from words spoken by Averell Harriman, who was American ambassador to Russia from 1943 to 1946.

Source 20e

An iron curtain has fallen across the continent. Behind it lie all the capitals of the states of central and eastern Europe. These great cities and their people are under the control of Moscow. This is not the free Europe that we fought to build up.

Adapted from a speech made by Winston Churchill in the U.S A. in 1946.

Source 20c

East German border defences between East Germany and West Berlin. They were there to stop East Germans escaping to West Berlin, and so to West Germany.

Source 20f

The Russians threw aside the goodwill that had been earned during the war. They tried to embarrass and weaken the democracies at every turn. They spoke of peace, but threatened war. Slowly, the West remembered that the aim of Communists was to spread world revolution.

Adapted from a book written by R. J. Unstead in 1963.

Exercise 20.4

Read **Sources 20b, 20d, 20e** and **20f**.

a **Sources 20b** and **20d** give one version of Stalin's thoughts, fears, and motives. Write a paragraph in your own words, saying
   i What Stalin was afraid of, and
   ii What he wanted to do about it.
b **Sources 20e** and **20f** tell us what a lot of people in the West thought about the Russians after 1945. Write a paragraph in your own words, saying
   i What had happened in eastern Europe, and
   ii What might happen elsewhere if the West did not take care.

21 Europe in Ruins

A street scene in Berlin just after the end of the war. The mother, Elsa Gabriele, has to share a pair of shoes with her neighbour. Her sons are carrying their shoes to avoid wearing them out!

A The results of war

Thirty million people died in the Second World War. When it ended, a large part of Europe was in ruins. Five million houses were destroyed in Russia, and the same number again in the rest of Europe. Some city streets were nothing but cleared paths between heaps of rubble. Berlin was almost a complete ruin. Cologne, Hamburg, Warsaw, and Budapest were much the same.

Broken bridges, pot-holed roads, and a shortage of petrol made travel difficult. The railways were worse than the roads — lines blown up, tunnels flooded, engines and trucks wrecked. In the countryside, farm buildings were smashed, and fields were scarred by the tracks of tanks.

In the first few months of peace, the food rations were reduced, not increased. In parts of Italy, bread was sold by the slice. For butter, eggs, and real coffee, you had to go to the **black market**. Farmers were growing less than before the war — the wheat crop of 1945 was only 60 per cent of the normal yield. Almost half the cattle and sheep had been killed in the war. And broken roads and railways stopped what food there was from reaching the towns.

As the war came to an end, **law and order** often broke down. Russian soldiers, it was said, were thieves and drunken beasts. Lynch-mobs took over for a while in parts of what had been occupied Europe. French men and women who had helped the Nazis were hanged or shot without trial. Girls who had been friendly with the Germans had their heads shaved and were put on public show.

Now try Exercises 21.1 and 21.2.

Source **21b**

A food queue in
Germany in 1946

After the allied forces
drove the Germans
out, the French
people turned on
men and women who
had been friendly
with the Germans.
Girlfriends of
German soldiers had
their heads shaved in
public.

Exercise 21.1

Read **Section A**. Copy these notes on the results of the war,
and fill in the blank spaces:

a People. _____ million people died.

b Houses. In the whole of Europe, _____ million
houses were destroyed.

c Transport. Road travel was difficult because _____
and _____ were damaged, and there was not
much _____. In many places, railway lines had
been _____. Railway _____ and trucks
had been destroyed.

d Food. Food was scarce, because _____ were
growing less, and many farm _____ had been
killed. Damaged _____ and _____ made
things worse.

e Law and order. Some _____ soldiers killed
and ill-treated Germans, and stole their goods. In countries
that had been _____ men and women who
had helped the Germans were often _____
without trial.

Exercise 21.2

Read **Source 21c**, and look at **Sources 21a** and **21b**. Answer the questions.

a What can you learn from **Source 21a** about
  i the state of the streets in Berlin soon after the end of the war
  ii life for ordinary Germans at that time?

b What can you learn from **Source 21b** about
  i food supplies
  ii people's clothes?

c What can you learn from **Source 21c** about
  i fuel supplies
  ii food rationing
  iii the black market?

Source 21c

The bathroom is freezing cold, and it is hard to wash without a drop of hot water. We wear our oldest clothes all day, coats on top, and nobody cares what you look like. The only things everyone cares about are the daily questions, 'Have you any coal? Have you any potatoes? Can you manage on the bread ration?' We have spent 1,000 marks on the black market, buying dripping, butter, and sugar. Money does not matter. All that matters is food and surviving through the coming winter.

Adapted from the diary of Mathilde Wolff-Mönckeberg. This passage was written on 16 November 1945.

B The refugees

The **refugees** were the grey-faced, shabbily dressed men, women, and children who shuffled along Europe's roads in the first weeks of peace. They carried parcels and bags, or pushed hand-carts or prams. These were their entire possessions — all that they had in the world. As they passed by, they scavenged or begged for food. At night, they found shelter in the ruins, and made fires from what had been doors or window frames.

They were called 'refugees' — people seeking refuge, somewhere safe, a place that they could call home. Some of them had fled from the fighting and air-raids. Some were survivors from concentration camps or forced-labour gangs. And about twelve million of the thirty million refugees were Germans who had been driven from their homes in Czechoslovakia or what was now Poland.

German refugees from the fighting make their way home in 1945

At first, it was the allied armies' job to care for the refugees. They put them in camps, and fed them as well as they could. Allied officers and men worked long and hard to find relatives who had survived. They helped as many as possible to make their way back home.

But the main work was done by **UNRRA**. (The letters stand for United Nations Relief and Rehabilitation Agency.) Most of UNRRA's money came from the U.S.A.. Its volunteer staff ran refugee camps and children's homes, gave out food and clothes, and organized repairs. They helped the refugees return to their homes or build new ones, and they put them back on their feet. And by the end of 1947, most of their work was done.

Now try Exercise 21.3.

Exercise 21.3

Read **Section B**. Find out the answers to these questions about the refugees. Write your answers either in sentences or in a short essay.

a Who were they?
b Where had they come from?
c How could you recognize them?
d What were their main problems?
e Who looked after them **i** at first **ii** later?
f What in the end happened to them?
g How long did it take to solve the refugee problem?

C Marshall Aid

In the first years of peace, Europe did not grow enough food to feed its hungry people. Also, its factories and mines produced less than before the war. As a result, the countries of Europe had less to sell to the rest of the world, so they did not earn the money to buy the extra food they needed.

Europe's weakness was bad for the U.S.A. The people of Europe were not selling much to the U.S.A., so they were not earning many dollars. Therefore, they could not afford to buy much from American firms. To get **trade** going again, President Truman lent dollars to Britain, France, Belgium, and Holland. Later, aid was sent to Greece and Turkey as well.

In 1947, the U.S. Secretary of State, **George Marshall**, went much further. He announced that the U.S.A. would **give** aid to any country in Europe. But the countries that took the aid had to play their part too. They had to work hard to restore their own industry, agriculture, and trade. Most of Western Europe gladly accepted 'Marshall Aid'. But Stalin said 'no', and he would not let his allies in Eastern Europe take part either.

Between 1948 and 1952, the U.S.A. sent **13,000 million dollars'** worth of Marshall Aid to Europe. Aid came in many forms — food, tractors, lorries, railway engines, etc. Never has a nation given so much away. All the time, the people of Europe were rebuilding from the ruins of war. Long before Marshall Aid came to an end, trade in Western Europe had doubled. By 1952, most parts of Western Europe were back on their feet.

Now try Exercise 21.4.

American 'CARE' parcels being handed out to hungry Germans in 1953

Source 21d

Stalin was very cautious. He had hoped for aid from the U.S.A. before, and had been disappointed. Now he was on his guard. He was suspicious of all the Western powers since they had turned against Russia. So he decided to have nothing to do with the Marshall Plan. He thought that it was part of an American scheme to control Europe and destroy Communism. And he told the other states of Eastern Europe to withdraw from the plan as well.

Based on a book written by Ian Grey in 1979. (Not Mr Grey's own words.)

Source 21e

When Mr. Marshall came along and said he was willing to consider a plan for Europe, I welcomed it. I felt that it was the first chance that we had been given since the end of the war to look at Europe's problems as a whole. ... I said to myself at once, 'It is up to us to tell them what we want. It is up to us to produce a plan. ... This is no time for delay — there is too much involved.'

Adapted from a speech made by Ernest Bevin, Britain's Foreign Secretary, in the House of Commons in June 1947.

Exercise 21.4

Read **Section C** and **Sources 21d** and **21e**. Read the sentences below, then write out those which you think are true.

a Stalin thought that Russia was too well off to need aid from the U.S.A.
b Stalin thought that the Marshall Plan was an American trap.
c Stalin thought that the Americans wanted to destroy Communism.
d Stalin did not want the U.S.A. to help the states of Eastern Europe.
e Ernest Bevin, like Stalin, was suspicious of the U.S.A.
f Bevin was too proud to accept American help.
g Bevin thought that the Marshall Plan was good news for Europe.
h Bevin thought that Britain would have to draw up a plan for recovery.
i Bevin's thoughts can be summed up in the words 'the sooner the better'.

22 The United Nations

A The birth of the United Nations

The League of Nations was the first attempt by the nations of the world to work together for peace. (See Chapter 5.) But the League of Nations failed, for two main reasons. The first was that it had no clear rules on how to prevent war. The second was that not all of the world's great powers belonged to it.

Early in 1942, statesmen from the twenty-six nations that were then on the allied side, met in **Washington**. They agreed that they were fighting for the same thing — the right of all men and women to life, freedom, and justice. And they hoped that, when peace was restored, all nations would join in keeping the peace and preserving these rights.

The next step came in **Moscow** in 1943. There the foreign ministers of the 'big three' powers (Russia, Britain, and the U.S.A.) met and decided to set up an organization to keep the peace. And they agreed that it would have to be stronger than the old League. Two meetings in the U.S.A. in 1944 and 1945 turned the idea into reality. At the second, in **San Francisco**, the **United Nations** came to life.

At San Francisco, the fifty-one nations that were by then on the side of the allies, signed the **Charter** of the United Nations. This was the UN's book of laws. It laid down how the members would settle their quarrels, and how they would deal with threats of war. And it said that the UN would work for human rights, justice, and prosperity throughout the world.

Now try Exercise 22.1.

Signing the United Nations Charter in 1945

Exercise 22.1

Read **Section A**. Then copy out the sentences, filling in the blank spaces.

a The statesmen who met at Washington in 1942 agreed that all people had a right to life, _____ and _____

b The same statesmen agreed that, after the war, all states should work together to keep the _____

c The foreign ministers of Russia, _____ and _____ met in Moscow in 1943.

d The United Nations was set up by a meeting of statesmen at _____ _____ in 1945.

e The _____ nations that were on the allied side in the war took part in this meeting.

f All of them signed the United Nations _____

g The U.N. Charter said that the aims of the United Nations were to settle _____, deal with threats of _____, and work for human _____

The U.N. headquarters building in New York

B The United Nations organization

The fifty-one nations which signed the Charter in 1945 were the first members of the United Nations. The Charter said that each of them would have a seat and a vote in the U.N.'s **General Assembly**. (Normally, the Assembly met, and still meets, once a year in New York.) In the years that followed, the number of members grew, but only slowly at first. By 1954, the U.N. still had only sixty-two members.

Dealing with disputes, keeping the peace, and stopping wars is the job of the U.N. **Security Council**. This is a smaller body than the Assembly. It meets when it is needed, and often at short notice.

The Security Council tries to get states to settle their quarrels with words, not bombs. If it thinks fit, it can send in **observers** to keep the hostile sides apart. If a war does start, it can condemn one side as the **aggressor** (the one who started the fighting). It can then instruct all U.N. members to punish the guilty state (e.g. by cutting off all trade). It can even ask members to use force to stop the war and restore peace.

In 1945, the Security Council had eleven members. (Now it has fifteen.) Five members were **permanent** — they had seats on the Council all the time. These were the great powers — the U.S.A., Russia, Britain, France, and China. The other six served for two years at a time. The permanent members had the power of **veto**. This meant that if one of them voted against a plan it had to be dropped, even if all the other states were in favour.

Now try Exercises 22.2 and 22.3.

The flag of the United Nations

Exercise 22.2

Read **Section B**. Find words and phrases in **Section B** which mean the same as the groups of words below:

a The United Nations book of rules or laws.
b The part of the United Nations where every member-state has a vote.
c The part of the United Nations which deals with keeping the peace.
d United Nations officers who find out what is happening in trouble-spots.
e The side which begins a war.
f Refusing to sell goods to a state, or to buy goods from it.
g States which always have a seat on the Security Council.
h The right to stop a plan by voting against it.

Source 22a

Exercise 22.3

Read **Source 22a**. Which of the points below is the U.N. for, and which is it against? Write out the list below, and after each word or phrase, write FOR or AGAINST.

a Equal rights for black, brown, and white people.
b Slavery.
c Torture.
d The right to a fair trial.
e The right to travel abroad.
f Women being forced to obey their husbands.
g The right to worship freely.
h Higher pay for men than women.
i Children having to go to school.

THE UNIVERSAL DECLARATION
OF Human Rights

1 *All human beings, regardless of race, colour, sex, or religion, are born free and have the same rights.*
2 *All people have the right to life and liberty.*
3 *Slavery and the slave trade shall be banned in all their forms.*
4 *No-one should suffer torture, or inhuman punishment. No-one should be put in prison without trial.*
5 *All people are equal before the law, and have the right to a fair trial.*
6 *All people have the right to travel freely in their own country. And they all have the right to leave their own country and return to it.*
7 *Adult men and women have the right to marry. Men and women are entitled to equal rights in marriage.*
8 *All people have the right to own property.*
9 *All people have the right to freedom of thought and religion, and to worship in freedom.*
10 *People have the right to take part in the government of their country.*
11 *All people have the right to work, and to equal pay for equal work.*
12 *Education should be free and compulsory.*

Some of the main points from the Universal Declaration of Human Rights, approved by the General Assembly of the United Nations on 10 December 1948. (Amended)

C The United Nations in action, 1945–1950

The right of veto (see Section B) means that if the great powers do not agree, the U.N. Security Council can do nothing. In the years 1945–1950, the great powers did not often agree. It was the Russians who were always out of step, voting 'no' when the others said 'yes'. Time after time, 'nyet' (the Russian for 'no') stopped the Council from doing its work.

The record of the Council was not all failure, though. In 1949, it brought peace to Kashmir, where India and Pakistan had been at war. And in the same year, it stopped a war between Israel and its Arab neighbours.

The worst problem at that time involved **China**. At the end of the war, the ruler of China was **Chiang Kai-shek**. He was an ally of the U.S.A., and his government had a permanent seat on the U.N. Security Council. But in 1948–1949 China had a civil war. **Mao Tse-tung**, who was a Communist and (at that time) a friend of Russia, took control.

Chiang Kai-shek fled to the island of **Formosa**. (Look at the map on page 100.) But he still called himself the ruler of China. And he kept his seat on the U.N. Security Council. The Russians said that this was wrong, and that Mao should have the Chinese seat. As a protest, they refused for a while in 1950 to attend the Council's meetings.

In June 1950, Communist **North Korea** attacked the non-Communist South. The Security Council agreed at once that this was an act of war. It asked the U.S.A. to send troops to help **South Korea**. (The Russians were absent from the Council, so they could not use their veto.) In the next three years, forces from sixteen states served under the U.N. flag in the Korean War. (Men from Mao's China fought on North Korea's side.) At the end of the war, the border was back at its original position.

Now try Exercise 22.4.

The U.N. Security Council in 1950. The empty chair was Russia's (See Section C).

This trick photograph shows American soldiers serving in South Korea. Behind them is a copy of the Security Council Resolution (decision) allowing member countries of the United Nations to send troops to help defend South Korea under the U.N. flag.

Exercise 22.4

Read **Section C**.

a Answer the following questions in sentences.

   i When can the United Nations Security Council do nothing?

   ii What stops the Security Council from taking action?

   iii Which of the great powers used the right of veto most often between 1945 and 1950?

   iv Which two wars did the Security Council manage to stop in 1949?

   v Who won the Chinese civil war?

   vi After 1949, who occupied China's place at the Security Council?

   vii What did the Russians say and do about this?

b Write a paragraph in your own words about the Korean war, saying

   i What the Security Council did when war broke out in Korea in 1950.

   ii Why the Russians were not able to stop the Security Council from taking South Korea's side.

   iii What the result was.

Key Elements and corresponding exercises (those printed in bold type are particularly relevant)

Key Element 1: Chronological knowledge and understanding

Chapters	1	2	3	4	5	6	7	8	9	10	11	12	13	14	15	16	17	18	19	20	21	22
a Historical knowledge	1.1	2.1	3.1	4.4	5.1	6.4	7.1	8.1	9.4	10.4	11.1	12.1	13.1	14.1	15.2	16.2	17.4	18.1	19.1	20.1	21.3	22.1 22.4
b Concepts and terminology		2.4		4.5	5.5	6.1			9.1				13.2				17.1		19.3			22.2
c Chronology	1.3							8.3	9.2			12.3						18.4				

Key Element 2: Range and depth of historical knowledge and understanding

	1	2	3	4	5	6	7	8	9	10	11	12	13	14	15	16	17	18	19	20	21	22
a Cause and consequence			**3.4**				**7.2**			10.3	11.4	**12.5**			15.4					20.2	21.1	
b Motivation										**10.1**			13.1	14.4		16.3						22.1
c Continuity and change			3.5	4.1																		
d Different features of situations	1.2								**9.5**		11.2	12.4					17.2	18.2				

Key Element 3: Awareness and understanding of interpretations of history

	1	2	3	4	5	6	7	8	9	10	11	12	13	14	15	16	17	18	19	20	21	22
a Different versions of events and topics			3.3			6.3	7.3							14.2			17.5					
b Recognizing fact and opinion		**2.5**		4.3	5.4	6.4						12.2			15.3	16.1	17.3					
c Different interpretations								**8.4**					13.4						19.4	20.4	21.4	

Key Element 4: Knowledge and understanding of the processes of historical enquiry

	1	2	3	4	5	6	7	8	9	10	11	12	13	14	15	16	17	18	19	20	21	22
a Acquiring information	1.4	2.3	3.2	4.2		6.4	7.4		9.3				13.3	14.5	15.5	16.4		18.1	19.2			
b Sources – authorship and dates			3.2		5.2							12.2		14.4			17.3				21.4	
c Primary and secondary sources					**5.2**			8.2		10.2	11.3	12.2		14.4	15.3	16.4						
d Making deductions from sources	1.4					**6.2**				10.1		12.4		14.3						20.3	21.2	22.3
e Using different kinds of source		2.2		4.2	5.3		7.4		9.3						15.1						21.2	
f Value and reliability of evidence								**8.2**		**10.2**	11.3							18.3	19.2			
g Collecting evidence														14.5	15.5							

Most of the exercises seek to develop organisational and communication skills (**Key Element 5**).